Slavery, Civil Rights, and Racism ENSL 0090

Academic English
Georgia Perimeter College

American Government Selections

Joseph R. Conlin | Benjamin G. Rader
Cal Jillson | Donelson R. Forsyth

Edited by
Mary Middlemas

Australia • Brazil • Japan • Korea • Mexico • Singapore • Spain • United Kingdom • United States

Slavery, Civil Rights, and Racism ENSL 0090: Academic English Georgia Perimeter College, American Government Selections

Joseph R. Conlin | Benjamin G. Rader
Cal Jillson | Donelson R. Forsyth

Edited by Mary Middlemas

Executive Editors:
Michele Baird
Maureen Staudt
Michael Stranz

Project Development Manager:
Linda deStefano

Senior Marketing Coordinators:
Sara Mercurio
Lindsay Shapiro

Production/Manufacturing Manager:
Donna M. Brown

PreMedia Services Supervisor:
Rebecca A. Walker

Rights & Permissions Specialist:
Kalina Hintz

Cover Image:
Getty Images*

* Unless otherwise noted, all cover images used by Custom Solutions, a part of Cengage Learning, have been supplied courtesy of Getty Images with the exception of the Earthview cover image, which has been supplied by the National Aeronautics and Space Administration (NASA).

ISBN-13: 978-0-534-09592-5

ISBN-10: 0-534-09592-5

Cengage Learning
5191 Natorp Boulevard
Mason, Ohio 45040
USA

Cengage Learning is a leading provider of customized learning solutions with office locations around the globe, including Singapore, the United Kingdom, Australia, Mexico, Brazil, and Japan. Locate your local office at:
international.cengage.com/region

Cengage Learning products are represented in Canada by Nelson Education, Ltd.

For your lifelong learning solutions, visit **custom.cengage.com**

Visit our corporate website at **cengage.com**

Printed in the United States of America

CONTENTS

Section One

"A Different Country: The South"

From Chapter 18 of *The American Past: A Survey of American History*

Pages 349-361

From *The American Past: A Survey of American History*, 6th edition, by Joseph R. Conlin, copyright 2001.

18

CHAPTER

A Different Country

The South

Practised in the Arts of Despotism and Cruelty, we become callous to the Dictates of Humanity, & all the other finer feelings of the Soul. Taught to regard a part of our Species in the most abject and contemptible Degree below us, we lose that Idea of the Dignity of Man, which the hand of Nature had implanted in us. . . . Habituated from our Infancy to trample upon the Rights of human Nature, every generous, every liberal Sentiment, if not extinguished, is enfeebled in our Mind. And in such an infernal School are to be educated our future Legislators and Rulers.

— *George Mason*

There must doubtless be an unhappy influence on the manners of our people produced by the existence of slavery among us. The whole commerce between master and slave is a perpetual exercise of the most boisterous passions, the most unremitting despotism on the one part, and degrading submissions on the other. Our children see this and learn to imitate it. . . . The parent storms, the child looks on, catches the lineaments of wrath, puts on the same airs in the circle of smaller slaves, gives loose to the worst of passions and thus nursed, educated, and daily exercised in tyranny, cannot but be stamped by it with odious peculiarities.

—*Thomas Jefferson*

Doodling at his desk one day, Thomas Jefferson drew up a list of character traits in which, he suggested, northerners and southerners differed. Northerners were cool and sober, he wrote, southerners were fiery and "voluptuary." Northerners were hard-working, self-interested, and chicaning (devious), southerners were lazy, generous, and candid. Northerners were "jealous of their own liberties, and just to those of others," southerners were "zealous for their own liberties, but trampling on those of others."

No doubt he had a point. Jefferson usually did, and it could not have been easy for him to tote up unattractive characteristics in his own people. (Never comfortably a nationalist, Jefferson referred to Virginia as "my country" until the day of his death.) Still, to fix upon the differences between the people of the North and the people of the South distorts the reality that they were much more alike than not. Southerners and northerners shared a common linguistic, religious, cultural, and political heritage. By 1826, the year of Jefferson's death, they also shared 50 years of national history.

Politically, North and South had inclined to line up on sectional lines. The Jefferson Republicans and Jackson's Democrats counted on a core of southern votes around which to build their majorities; the Federalists, National Republicans, and Whigs on their primacy in the New England states. Nevertheless, Jefferson and Jackson won the presidency only because they attracted many northern votes, too, while the Whigs competed with the Democrats as equals in the South until the 1850s. Zachary Taylor, one of only two Whigs elected president, was from Louisiana.

Despite the perturbation in South Carolina over the tariffs of 1828 and 1832, neither import duties, internal improvements, nor the question of a national bank seriously threatened the federal union.

SOUTHERN ANTISLAVERY

Until the 1830s, slavery was not a particularly divisive issue between the people of the two sections. The institution was abolished or in the process of elimination in the North, while it remained a buttress of southern society. Still, New Yorkers did not finally abandon the institution until 1827, and there were some slaves in New Jersey—all quite legal—as late as 1860. Except in a few states like Massachusetts and New Hampshire, where slavery was abolished at a blow in the Revolutionary Era, middle-aged northerners could tell the young firsthand of the days when there were slaves among them. Few northerners regretted doing away with the institution. Equally few found the fact that southerners clung to slavery to be intolerable.

Manumission and Race

In fact, until the 1830s, the future of slavery was an open question in the South. Many of the most powerful southerners, the very people who owed their wealth, leisure, and status to the forced labor of their human property, worried openly about the undesirable social, economic, and moral consequences of the institution. Thomas Jefferson agonized over slavery to the end of his life. It caused no disturbance when wealthy planters manumitted—freed—their slaves in their wills. George Washington was honored for doing so. George Wythe and Jefferson also freed some slaves in their wills. Less celebrated southerners frequently rewarded individual slaves with freedom for extraordinary services. In 1833, Virginian John Randolph freed 400 blacks with a stroke of his pen, the largest single manumission in American history.

The possibility of abolition—legal prohibition of slavery—arose several times in the states of the upper South. But, in the end, every state below the Mason-Dixon line and the Ohio River opted to preserve the institution. The decisive factors were the beliefs about race that were, simply, the assumption of the era. Most white southerners (and white northerners, for that matter) sincerely believed that blacks, as a people, were their innate inferiors in intelligence, initiative, and even moral fiber.

Jefferson's Bequest

Like many planters, Jefferson freed some slaves in his will. Sally Hemmings, whom Jefferson's enemies claimed was his mistress, was not among them. She was bequeathed to Jefferson's daughter, Patsy. Does this give the lie to the attacks on Jefferson? Some historians think not. They point out that Virginia required manumitted slaves to leave the state. To have freed Sally Hemmings, who was well along in years in 1826, would have forced her to leave her lifelong friends and children.

Read 351-354

Southern Success Story

In 1841, John Hampden Randolph purchased a plantation in Iberville Parish (county), Louisiana. The price was astronomical, $30,000, but the down payment was only $863, the odd amount implying that Randolph was not rich in cash. He paid off the mortgage by planting cotton, but then switched to sugar. Before the outbreak of the Civil War, Randolph owned several thousand acres and 195 slaves. His sons were university educated, and he sent his daughters to a finishing school in Baltimore. In 1858, he built a 51-room mansion, Nottoway, which survives.

It was one thing for northerners holding such views to set blacks free. The black population was numerically insignificant in most northern states. In 1830, there were 125,000 blacks in the Northeast, amidst a total population of 5.54 million. There were but 42,000 blacks in the states of the Old Northwest, with 1.6 million people. So small a minority could be ignored, disdained, and pushed aside to root or die, as northern blacks were. There was no concern that their perceived undesirable traits would overwhelm the culture. The black population was not a social problem.

But blacks were the backbone of the agricultural workforce in the South, and a substantial part of the population, 2.16 million in 1830 as compared to 3.54 million whites. If such numbers, firmly under control as slaves, were suddenly or even gradually freed to compete with poor whites at the bottom of southern society, southerners who thought about the question usually concluded the result would be profound cultural decay, social dislocation, even chaos. The

Although this photograph was taken after the Civil War, the scene would have been much the same in 1830 or 1840.

How They Lived

The Republic of Porkdom

Today, a good many Americans would regard a tender corn-fed filet mignon as the *ne plus ultra* of fine eating. The ground-beef hamburger comes as close to being a national dish as is possible in a pluralistic society. Beef is unquestionably America's favorite meat; Americans consume almost two pounds of it to every pound of pork, including bacon and ham, that they eat.

Americans of the early nineteenth century prized beef too, but, while they ate quite as much meat per capita as we do, beef was far less common on their tables than pork. Indeed, according to a writer in *Godey's Lady's Book*—the combination *Ladies Home Journal, Ms.*, and *Vogue* of the era—put it,

> The United States of America might properly be called the great Hog-eating Confederacy, or the Republic of Porkdom. [In the] South and West . . . it is fat bacon and pork, fat bacon and pork only, and that continually morning, noon, and night, for all classes, sexes, ages, and conditions; and except the boiled bacon and collards at dinner, the meat is generally fried, and thus supersaturated with grease in the form of hog's lard.

Even slaves on well-managed plantations were provided with half a pound of salt pork a day.

Beef was less common, first of all, because it was relatively much more expensive than it is today. Cattle had to be transported on the hoof, which meant that cities could be supplied only from the near hinterland. Farmers on comparatively expensive real estate in the older states could generally do better cultivating their land than leaving it in pasture. Only with the development of the Great Plains after the Civil War did the price of beef decline. Even then, in 1900 Americans ate as much pork as beef.

Unlike cattle, hogs flourished on wasteland, multiplying their weight 150 times in eight months on nuts and roots in the woods, fallen orchard fruit unfit for consumption, harvested gardens and grain fields, and offal—garbage. They required next to no attention. Indeed, the "bony, snake-headed, hairy wild beasts," the American "razorback," needed no protection. (A farmer's fields and the farmer himself needed protection from them!)

Hogs were ideally suited to a nation where land was abundant and labor was scarce, and they thrived. As early as 1705, Robert Beverley wrote in his *History of Virginia* that "hogs swarm like Vermine upon the Earth, and are often accounted such. . . . When an Inventory of any considerable Man's Estate is taken, the Hogs are left out." In the southern states in 1850, there were two hogs for each human being.

Hogs had another recommendation over steers. They could be slaughtered where they were raised and cheaply preserved, butchered, and packed in salty brine in barrels to keep for a year or to be shipped to urban markets. Salt deposits were very important to early western pioneers because of the necessity of preserving pork. Cities on the Ohio and Mississippi Rivers, such as Cincinnati and St. Louis, owed much of their growth to their role as meat packers. Poor people owed their survival to salt pork. "I hold a family to be in a desperate way," a character in a James Fenimore Cooper novel put it, "when the mother can see the bottom of the pork barrel."

Scraping the bottom of the barrel is not the only catch phrase that survives in the language from the days of the Republic of Porkdom. We still use the term *pork barrel bill* to describe those congressional enactments, usually rushed through at the end of a session, that spend federal money in just about every district in which incumbents from the majority party are up for election—a highway improvement here, an agricultural station there, a defense installation somewhere else. The phrase conveys an image once familiar to every American—the none-too-pleasant appearance of chunks of pork bobbing about in a barrel of brine.

South's propertyless "po' white trash" was enough of a worry to thoughtful social conservatives; the idea of two million destitute free blacks caused them nightmares.

Before about 1830, there was little that was malicious or apocalyptic in southern statements along these lines. In fact, there was a melancholy sense of fatefulness in southern ruminations. In continuing

to hold blacks as slaves, many planters of the late eighteenth and early nineteenth centuries believed, they were not so much preserving their own wealth and social standing as they were shouldering a tragic burden that was strapped to their backs by history. They were protecting the blacks from the hostility of poor whites; they were preserving their society from anarchy.

The Colonization Movement

The American Colonization Society, founded in 1817, tried to provide troubled southerners with an alternative to the "blot" of slavery on the one hand and chaos on the other. With the active support of such distinguished southerners as Bushrod Washington, Francis Scott Key, Presidents Madison and Monroe, John Marshall, and Henry Clay, the society proposed to raise money with which free blacks would be transported to West Africa. By ridding the South of free blacks, the advocates of colonization believed, they would avert racial conflict, encourage individual slave owners to free their human property, and prompt state legislatures to adopt laws abolishing the undesirable institution. Idealism was not the society's strong point; it described the free black population as "for the most part idle and useless, and too often vicious and mischievous."

Congress voted the Society $100,000 in seed money and, in 1820, it financed the emigration of a few former slaves to Sierra Leone, a colony established by the British as a refuge for blacks freed from bondage within the British Empire. The society then purchased a stretch of African coastline south of Sierra Leone and helped establish the black Republic of Liberia, with its capital at Monrovia (named for President James Monroe). All told, about 11,000 American blacks settled in Liberia. They established a government patterned on the American model and, less happily, reduced the native people of the region to a kind of servitude with themselves on top.

Colonization proved an unrealistic program. There were 1.5 million slaves in the United States in 1820, and 2 million in 1830, far more people than could be colonized on a small strip of African seacoast. Moreover, few free blacks were interested in going to Africa. Most were generations removed from their African roots—which were rarely in Liberia in any case—and felt no attraction to an unknown land. Virginia, Georgia, and Arkansas may not have been hospitable homes, but homes they were. West Africa was not.

As for southern whites, the longer the price of cotton boomed on the world market, the less was heard about the antislavery aspects of colonization. When the Mississippi Colonization Society was founded in 1829, its pronounced purpose was to rid the state of free blacks. Its officers disassociated themselves from the old goal of encouraging planters to free their slaves. Even in the upper South, where little cotton was grown, the profitability of selling surplus slaves down the river dulled the appeal of

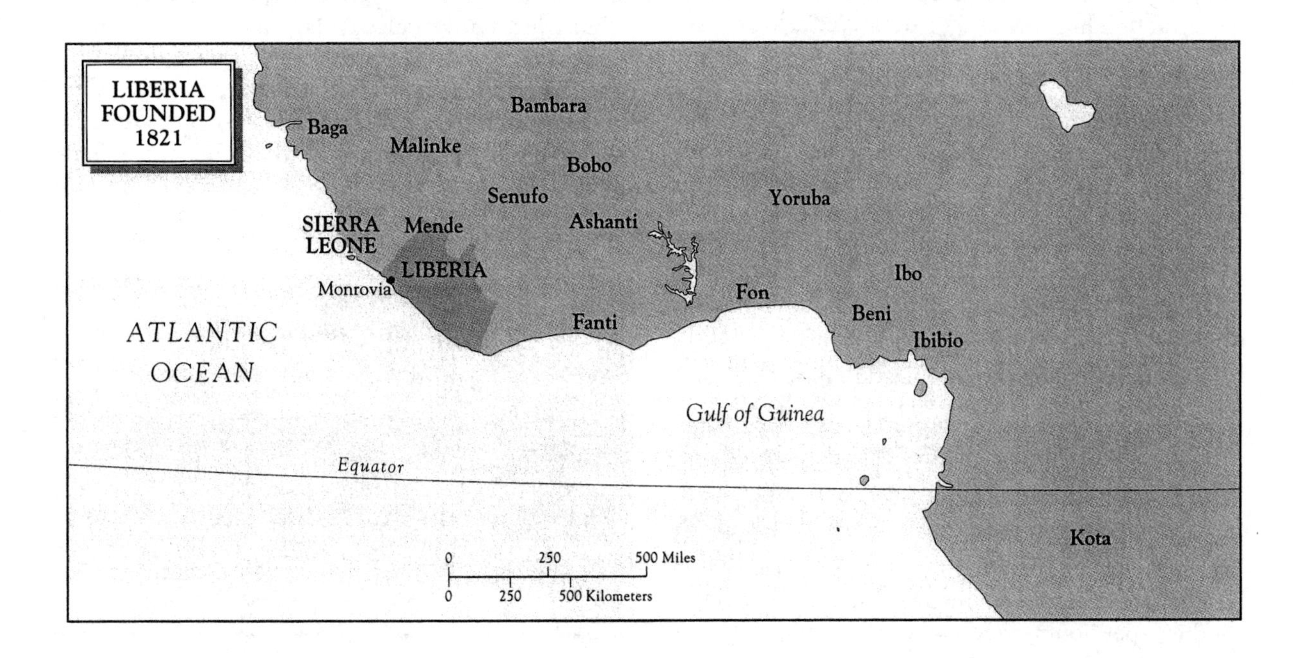

Where Is Home?

In 1822, James Forten commented sarcastically on the proposal of the American Colonization Society to pay the way of people like him "back to Africa."

My great-grandfather was brought to this country a slave from Africa. My grandfather obtained his own freedom. My father never wore the yoke. He rendered valuable service to his country in the war of our Revolution; and I, though then a boy, was a drummer in that war. I have since lived and labored in a useful employment, have acquired property, and have paid taxes. . . . Yet some ingenious gentlemen have recently discovered that I am still an African; that a continent, three thousand miles away—and more—from the place where I was born is my native country.

colonization. Except for one last debate, by 1830 the southern antislavery movement was dead.

The Last Debate

In December 1831, Governor John Floyd of Virginia asked the legislature to consider a plan to phase out slavery over a period of years. Slave owners were to be compensated for their losses; for the good of the state, taxpayers would accommodate those who lost property, just as if real estate were taken for the purposes of building a road. For three weeks in January 1832, the delegates discussed the proposal, for the most part moderately and intelligently.

Even the staunchest proslavery men were defensive. Typically, they introduced their speeches by regretting the fact that blacks were ever brought to Virginia, and by saying that the state would be a better place if it were developed by free white labor. However, they also concluded that the past was history; blacks constituted about half of Virginia's population; so large a population of free blacks was out of the question; and the colonization movement was obviously a failure. However tragic it was for the Old Dominion, Virginia must continue to be a slave state.

The assumption that a biracial society would not work carried the day—but just barely. At the end of January, the legislature rejected the Floyd plan by 73 to 58. A switch of only eight votes would have altered the course of American history, for the other states of the upper South—Delaware, Maryland, and Kentucky—could not have ignored abolition in Virginia. Had those states phased slavery out, slavery would not have split the Union across the middle. It would have been the peculiar institution of a few, generally lightly populated states in the Deep South. As it was, once the Virginia debate was over, no powerful party of southern whites ever again considered the possibility of ridding themselves of the institution.

THREATS TO THE SOUTHERN ORDER

Both Floyd's proposal and the Virginia legislature's rejection of it were profoundly influenced by two events that electrified the South in 1831: the appearance in the North of a new kind of antislavery agitator, and an uprising of slaves in Southampton County, Virginia, under the leadership of Nat Turner.

Early Abolitionists

While the mainstream debate over slavery revolved around its political justice, economic wisdom, and social consequences, there had always been a few voices raised about the morality of human bondage. Some eighteenth-century Quakers, such as John Woolman of New Jersey and Anthony Benezet of Philadelphia, spoke publicly of the sinfulness of slavery. Benjamin Lay wrote a pamphlet called *All Slave-Keepers Apostates* and once kidnapped the child of a slave-owning Quaker for a day as an object lesson in what whites did to blacks. During the 1820s, Benjamin Lundy called for gradual abolition and the colonization of blacks in Haiti, Canada, or Texas (then a part of Mexico). Educated black people, notably the mathematician and astronomer Benjamin Banneker, published moral arguments against slavery

Calhoun's Consistency

When abolitionists quoted the Declaration of Independence to proslavery southerners—"all men are created equal"—the southerners were generally forced to make convoluted interpretations of the phrase in order to excuse slavery. John C. Calhoun, at least, was consistent. "Taking the proposition literally," he said, "there is not a word of truth in it."

and drew support from white religious groups and communities of free blacks in both North and South.

With few exceptions (like Benjamin Lay), these abolitionists treated the subject as one to be discussed calmly and moderately, in terms of one Christian concerned about the soul of another. Their fraternal attitude toward slave owners was typified by the Boston Unitarian William Ellery Channing, who told southerners, "We consider slavery your calamity and not your curse." None of them used language as harsh as had Virginians Thomas Jefferson or John Randolph in excoriating slavery.

David Walker and William Lloyd Garrison

In 1829, language and mood took on new forms. In that year, a free black dealer in cloth living in Boston, David Walker, published a pamphlet called *The Appeal.* After reviewing the traditional arguments about the immorality and injustice of slavery, Walker stated that unless whites abolished the institution, blacks had a moral duty to rise up in violent rebellion.

William Lloyd Garrison, a spare, intense young white man of 24, who was working for Benjamin Lundy in Baltimore, did not believe in violent rebellion. Among the many evangelical reform movements he supported was pacifism, or opposition to all wars. And yet, when Garrison founded his antislavery newspaper *The Liberator,* in Boston in January 1831, his language was belligerent and incendiary, and aimed not only at the institution of slavery—the sin—but at the sinners, slave owners. In the first issue of his paper Garrison wrote:

> I am aware that many object to the severity of my language; but is there not cause for severity? I will be as harsh as truth, and as uncompromising as justice. On this subject I do not wish to

The Philadelphia Anti-Slavery Society, 1851. Lucretia Coffin is seated second from the right.

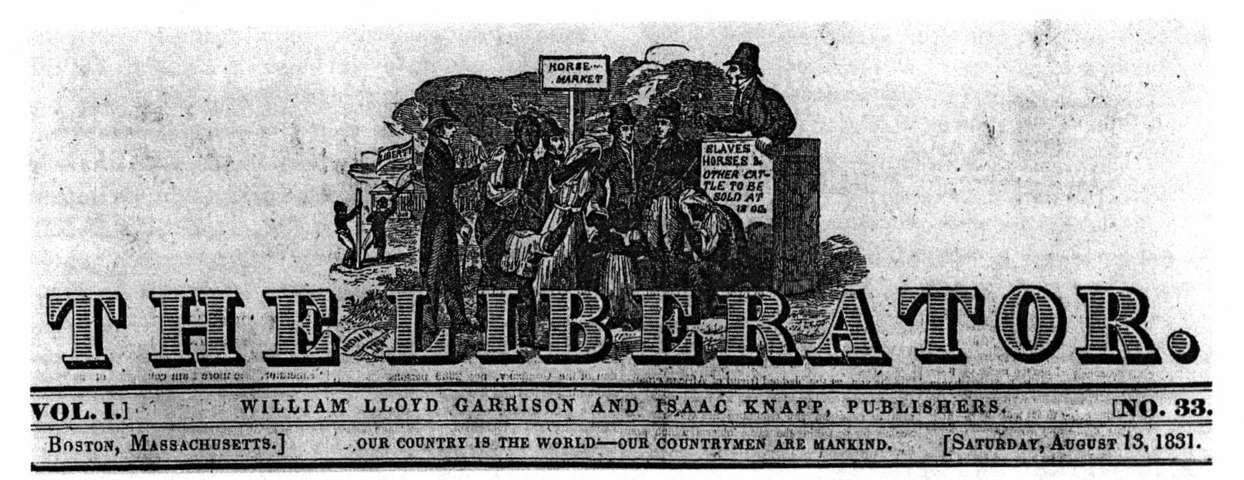

The masthead of William Lloyd Garrison's antislavery newspaper.

> think, or speak, or write, with moderation. No! No! Tell a man whose house is on fire to give a moderate alarm; tell him to moderately rescue his wife from the hands of the ravisher; tell the mother to gradually extricate her babe from the fire into which it has fallen;—but urge me not to use moderation in a cause like the present.

It was a declaration of war. To Garrison, the day of discourse and compromise was done. Slavery was evil, pure and simple; slave owners and those who accommodated them were doers of evil. Garrison described the slave owner's life as "one of unbridled lust, of filthy amalgamation, of swaggering braggadocio, of haughty domination, of cowardly ruffianism, of boundless dissipation, of matchless insolence, of infinite self-conceit, of unequaled oppression, of more than savage cruelty."

This sort of thing does not usually go down well with the subjects of it. Indeed, Garrison was even unpopular in the North. (He would have been wracked with doubt that the devil was in him had he been a mass hero.) Even in Boston, a center of antislavery sentiment, Garrison was hooted and pelted with stones when he spoke in public. On one occasion, a mob threw a noose around his neck and dragged him through the streets. He was rescued only when the aggressiveness of a group of abolitionist women momentarily shocked the mob. (Garrison was also a supporter of women's rights.)

In the South, Garrison was regarded as a monster. Not because he was against slavery, at least not at first: antislavery southerners loathed him as intensely as did proslavery southerners. Garrison and other extremist abolitionists were hated because they were believed to be inciting bloody slave rebellion. In 1831, the fear of slave rebellion in the South was no abstract speculation.

Nat Turner

Nat Turner, a slave of Southampton County, Virginia, was a queer amalgam of mystic dreamer and hardheaded realist. Literate—unusual among slaves—he pored over the Bible, drawing his own interpretations of its meaning. The rebellion he led in August and September 1831 was triggered by a solar eclipse that he took as a sign from God. And yet, Turner's revolt had a very practical goal—personal liberty—and Turner had a realistic conception of the

WANTED: Nat Turner

Five feet 6 or 8 inches high, weighs between 150 and 160 pounds, rather bright complexion, but not a mulatto. Broad shoulders, large flat nose, large eyes. Broad flat feet, rather knock-kneed, walks brisk and active. Hair on the top of the head very thin, no beard, except on the upper lip and at the top of the chin. A scar on one of his temples, also one at the back of his neck. A large knot on one of the bones of his right arm, near his wrist, produced [by] a blow.

odds that faced him. He planned with care, divulging his scheme to only a few trusted friends who swore with him to fight to the death. On the night of August 21, 1831, armed with little more than farm tools, the little group moved like lightning. They swept across Southampton County, killing 60 whites and recruiting more supporters from among the slaves.

The rising was over quickly, but before the rebels were rounded up after six weeks in hiding, there were 70 in their band. Forty, including Nat Turner, were hanged. Others, who were not directly responsible for spilling blood, were sold out of state. Undoubtedly, other blacks, including the innocent, were murdered by angry or frightened whites who did not bother to report the deaths. Law officers were not in a mood to work to rule.

The Fear of Rebellion

Turner's rebellion was not the first to throw a scare into white southerners. In 1800, a black man named Gabriel Prosser plotted an uprising in Richmond that may have passively involved as many as a thousand slaves. In 1822, a free black carpenter in Charleston, Denmark Vesey, tried to organize a conspiracy to murder whites, burn the city, and flee to Haiti. Also, runaway slaves in Georgia joined with Seminole Indians to raid outlying plantations and free the slaves there. At one time or another, planters in every part of the South suspected slaves of plotting rebellion.

No doubt many of the suspected plots were figments of overwrought imaginations; but there was nothing imaginary about Nat Turner, and a tremor of fear ran through the white South. In some parts of Louisiana, Mississippi, and South Carolina, blacks outnumbered whites by 20 to 1. Mary Boykin Chesnut, a South Carolinian of the planter class, was not observing a demographic curiosity when she described her family's plantation at Mulberry as "half a dozen whites and sixty or seventy Negroes, miles away from the rest of the world."

If many white southerners shared such anxieties, their belief in black inferiority meant that few were willing to admit that blacks, left to their own devices, were capable of mounting a rebellion. To white southerners, it was no coincidence that Turner's uprising followed the fiery first issue of *The Liberator* by only eight months. They took note of the fact that Turner knew how to read, and so they blamed antislavery propagandists like Garrison for the tragedy.

SOUTHERNERS CLOSE RANKS

Once Virginians decided that the Old Dominion would remain a slave state, the South stood almost alone in the western world. The northern states had abolished the institution. The Spanish-speaking republics of the Americas had done so, too. Great Britain was in the process of emancipating the slaves in its colonies. In the entire Christian world, slavery survived only in the Spanish colonies of Cuba and Puerto Rico and the independent Empire of Brazil.

After 1832, southerners faced up to the fact that American Negro slavery was a peculiar institution, a way of life almost unique to them, and they moved on three fronts to protect it. First, they insulated the South from outside ideas that threatened slavery, and they suppressed dissent at home. Second, white southerners ceased to apologize to themselves and others for slavery. Instead of calling it a historical tragedy or a necessary evil, they devised the argument that slavery was a positive good that benefited slave owner, slave, and society as a whole. Third, they reformed the state slave codes (the laws that governed the peculiar institution), both improving the material conditions under which slaves lived and instituting stricter controls over the black population.

Southern Anxieties

Both antislavery and proslavery southerners feared slave rebellion. The chief difference between them was in the tone in which they spoke of blacks.

Thomas Ritchie, an antislavery Virginian: "To attempt to excite discontent and revolt, or publish writings having this tendency, obstinately and perversely, among us, is outrageous—it ought not to be passed over with indifference. Our own safety—the good and happiness of our slaves, requires it."

Edward D. Holland, a proslavery South Carolinian: "Let it never be forgotten that our NEGROES are truly the *Jacobins* of the country; that they are the *anarchists* and the *domestic enemy*, the *common enemy of civilized society*, and the barbarians who would, IF THEY COULD, become the DESTROYERS of our race."

Suppression of Dissent

Most southern states passed laws that forbade the distribution of abolitionist literature within their borders. Officials screened the federal mails and seized copies of *The Liberator*, other antislavery newspapers, and books. Georgia's legislature actually offered a reward of $5,000 to any person who would bring William Lloyd Garrison into the state to stand trial for inciting rebellion.

Even if the resolution were meant to be symbolic, a state legislature's willingness to sanction a felony illustrates the depth of bitterness in the South toward abolitionists. David Walker was murdered, found poisoned in his shop. In border states like Kentucky, abolitionists such as John Gregg Fee and the politician Cassius Marcellus Clay (a relative of Henry) were generally unmolested, but they were the exception. The expression of antislavery opinions was no longer acceptable below the Mason-Dixon line.

Nor even in Washington, beginning in 1836, southern congressmen annually nagged the House of Representatives to adopt a rule providing that every petition dealing with slavery that the House received be tabled, set aside with no discussion on the floor. Former President John Quincy Adams, now a member of Congress, argued that this gag rule violated the right to free speech. Adams was not an abolitionist. He considered crusaders like Walker and Garrison to be dangerous and irresponsible fanatics. But he insisted on the constitutional right of abolitionists to be heard, and because he criticized southerners for quashing the right of petition, the lifelong nationalist came to be lumped with the abolitionists as an enemy.

Positive Good

Shortly after Virginia's debate on the future of slavery, a professor of economics at the College of William and Mary, Thomas Roderick Dew, published a systematic defense of the slave system as a better way of organizing and controlling labor than the wage system of the North. By 1837, most southern political leaders were parroting and embroidering on Dew's theories. In the Senate, John C. Calhoun declared that compared with other systems by which racial and class relationships were governed,

Slaves beside their living quarters in South Carolina.

Racism in Scripture

Defenders of slavery were hard pressed when abolitionists quoted the Bible on the equality of all men and women before God. A few went so far as to answer that blacks were a different species from whites, even though it was known that mating between species produces sterile offspring and the children of mixed parents in the South were both numerous and fertile.

Southerners were more comfortable when they went to the Bible. They quoted the story of Noah's son Ham, who had humiliated his father and was therefore cursed when Noah said, "a servant of servants shall he be unto his brethren." Blacks were human beings, proslavery southerners agreed, but their race was "the mark of Ham." As Ham's descendants, they were doomed by God to be (borrowing from another source) "hewers of wood and drawers of water."

"the relation now existing in the slaveholding states is, instead of an evil, a good—a positive-good."

The proslavery argument included religious, historical, cultural, and social proofs of the justice and beneficence of the institution. The Bible, the positive-good propagandists argued, sanctioned slavery. Not only did the ancient Hebrews own slaves with God's blessing, but Christ had told a servant who wanted to follow him to return to his master and practice Christianity as a slave.

Dew and others pointed out that the great civilizations of antiquity, Greece and Rome, were slaveholding societies. Hardly barbaric in their eyes, slavery had served as the foundation of high culture since the beginning of recorded time. Slavery made possible the existence of a gracious and cultured upper class that, with its leisure, guarded the highest refinements of human achievement.

Southern planters took pride in the fact that, although elementary and secondary education in the South was inferior to that provided by the public school systems of the North, more upper-class southerners were college-educated than members of the northern elite. Even as late as 1860, there were more than 6,000 college students in Georgia, Alabama, and Mississippi and fewer than 4,000 in the New England states, which were, altogether, more populous.

As an aristocracy, southerners said, the planters were closer to the tradition of the gentlemanly founding fathers than were the vulgar, money-grubbing capitalists of the North. Because gentlemen dominated politics in the South, the section was far better governed than was the North, where demagogues from the dregs of society could win election by playing on the whims of the mob. Some planters liked to think of themselves as descended from the cavaliers of seventeenth-century England. The South's favorite author was Sir Walter Scott, who spun tales of flowering knighthood and chivalry.

George Fitzhugh, Sociologist

But did all these proofs justify denying personal freedom to human beings? Yes, answered George Fitzhugh, a Virginia lawyer, in two influential books: *A Sociology for the South* (1854) and *Cannibals All!* (1857). He amassed statistics and other evidence with which he argued that the southern slave lived a better material and social life than did the northern wage worker or the European peasant.

Like Dew and Calhoun, Fitzhugh argued that someone had to perform the drudgery in every society. In the South, menial work was done by slaves who were cared for from cradle to grave. Not only did the slave owner feed, clothe, and house his workers, but he also supported slave children, the injured and the disabled, and the elderly—all of whom were nonproductive. Fitzhugh delighted to point out that by comparison, the northern wage worker was paid only as long as there was work to be done and the worker fit to do it. The wage worker who was injured was cut loose to fend for himself in an uncaring world. His children, the elderly, and the incompetent were no responsibility of capitalist employers.

Consequently, the North was plagued by social problems that were unknown in the South. The North teemed with obnoxious, nattering reformers. The lower classes were irreligious and, in their misery, tumultuous. The free working class was tempted by socialistic, communistic, and other doctrines that threatened the social order. By comparison, Fitzhugh claimed, southern slaves were contented, indeed happy. "A merrier being does not exist on the face of the globe," Fitzhugh wrote, "than the Negro slave of the United States."

Management

Fitzhugh equated happiness with the material conditions of slave life—housing, clothing, diet—and compared them favorably with the conditions under which the poorest wage workers of the North lived. By the 1850s, when he wrote, most southern state legislatures had defined minimum living standards as part of their slave codes, and magazines like the *Southern Agriculturalist* regularly featured exchanges among slave owners about how well they treated their people.

The most commonly stated reason for keeping slaves adequately housed, clothed, and fed was practical: a healthy slave worked more efficiently and was less likely to rebel or run away. Also underlying the trend toward improvement in the conditions of slave life after the 1830s was the South's determination to give the lie to the abolitionists' depiction of slavery as a life of unremitting horror. Planters who did provide decent accommodations for their slaves took pleasure in showing slave quarters to northern or foreign visitors. They reassured themselves that they were just the beneficent patriarchs that the positive-good writers described. Less likely to be trumpeted were the measures of control that were devised in the wake of the Turner rebellion.

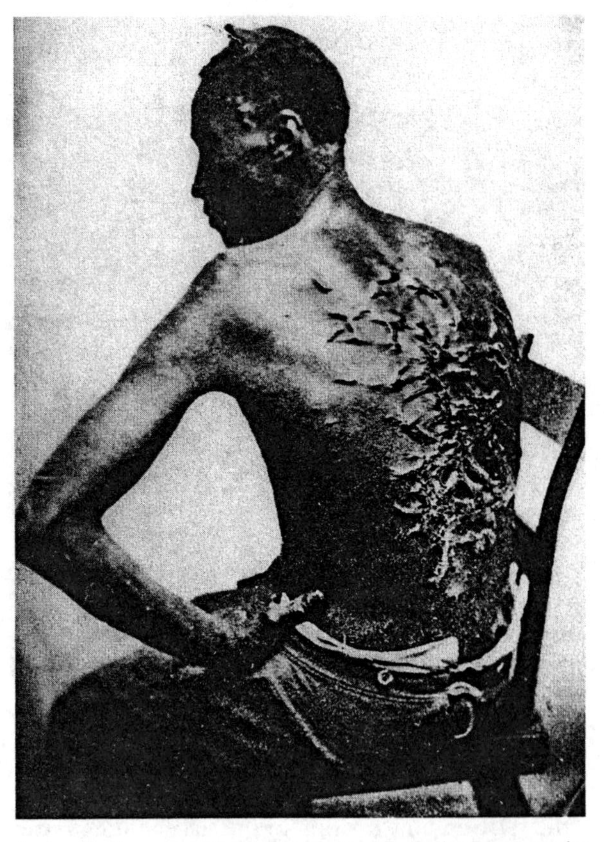

A slave displays scars from a brutal whipping. Such extreme cruelty was unusual, but many, perhaps most, slaves were whipped at one time or another.

Control

By 1840, the states of the Deep South had adopted laws that made it extremely difficult for a slave owner to free his slaves. Virginia required recently freed blacks to leave the state. (The law was impossible to enforce effectively.) It was also a crime in some southern states to teach a slave to read.

County governments were required to fund and maintain slave patrols. These mounted posses of armed whites policed the roads and plantations, particularly at night. They had the legal right to break into slave cabins or demand at gunpoint that any black (or white) account for himself or herself. Usually rough, hard-bitten men who were so poor that they sorely needed the undesirable job, the "paddyrollers" (patrollers) were brutal even with unoffending slaves and African Americans who were free. Black people hated and feared them. Their mere presence and arrogance cast a cloud of repression over the plantation regions that few outsiders failed to notice.

Blacks who were not under the direct supervision of their masters or overseers were required by law to carry written passes that gave them permission to be abroad, even just a mile or two from their cabins. Free blacks—there were about 250,000 in the South by 1860, 1 to every 15 slaves—also had to protect carefully the legal evidence of their status. Kidnappings of free blacks, and sale of them as slaves elsewhere in the South, were far from unknown.

The presence of free blacks presented a serious ideological problem for slave owners. One of the most effective means of controlling the slaves was to convince them that God and nature intended them to be slaves because of their race, and that they should be thankful to be under the care of their masters. But if slaves saw free blacks prospering, the argument flew to pieces. Slave owners also thought that free blacks were likely to stir up discontent among slaves, and they were probably right.

Religion could be an effective means of control, and careful masters paid close attention to the kind of preaching their property heard. Some owners took their slaves to their own churches where the minister was expected to deliver a sermon now and then based on biblical stories such as that of Hagar: "The angel of the Lord said unto her, return to Thy mistress, and submit thyself under her hands." Other masters permitted the blacks, who preferred an emotional Christianity enhanced with vestiges of West African culture, to have preachers of their own race. But these often eloquent men were instructed—specifically or indirectly—to steer clear of any topics that might cast doubt on the justice of slavery. Some toed the line. Others conveyed their protest by placing heavy emphasis on the ancient Israelites' bondage in Egypt and Babylon—and their ultimate deliverance. The idealized institution of John C. Calhoun and George Fitzhugh bore only an accidental relationship to slavery as it actually existed.

CHRONOLOGY

1817 American Colonization Society Founded

1822 Colonization Society purchases Liberia

1829 David Walker's *Appeal* is published

1831 Virginia legislature debates abolishing slavery
The Liberator commences publication
Turner's rebellion in southern Virginia

1836 Congress begins voting "gag rule" forbidding consideration of petitions concerning slavery

1854 Publication of George Fitzhugh's *Sociology for the South*

FOR FURTHER READING

On the South and its distinctive characteristics, see Avery O. Craven, *The Growth of Southern Nationalism, 1848–1860*, 1953; Clement Eaton, *The Growth of Southern Civilization*, 1961, and *A History of the Old South*, 1975; I. A. Newby, *The American South*, 1979; and Charles S. Sydnor, *The Development of Southern Sectionalism, 1819–1848*, 1948. Few historians today would subscribe to the conclusions in Wilbur Cash, *The Mind of the South*, 1940, and yet it contains many perceptive insights. A contemporary "travel book" about the Old South well worth reading is Frederick Law Olmstead, *The Cotton Kingdom*, 1861. See also James Oakes, *Slavery and Freedom: An Interpretation of the Old South*, 1990.

Of more specific concern but vital to understanding the subject are Edward A. Ayers, *Vengeance and Justice: Crime and Punishment in the Nineteenth-Century American South*, 1984; Dickson D. Bruce, *Violence and Culture in the Antebellum South*, 1979; Victoria E. Bynum, *Unruly Women: The Politics of Social and Sexual Control in the Old South*, 1992; William J. Cooper, *The South and the Politics of Slavery, 1828–1856*, 1978; Elizabeth Fox-Genovese, *Within the Plantation Household*, 1988; John Hope Franklin, *The Militant South*, 1956; Eugene Genovese, *The Political Economy of Slavery*, 1962, and *The World the Slaveholders Made*, 1969; Patrick Gerster and William Cords, eds., *Myth and Image in Southern History*, 1974; Fred Bateman and Thomas Weiss, *A Deplorable Scarcity: The Failure of Industrialism in the Slave Economy*, 1981; Bertram Wyatt-Brown, *Southern Honor: Ethics and Behavior in the Old South*, 1982; James Oakes, *The Ruling Race: A History of American Slaveholders*, 1982; Frank Owsley, *Plain Folk of the Old South*, 1949; William R. Taylor, *Cavalier and Yankee: The Old South and American National Character*, 1961; and Gavin Wright, *The Political Economy of the Cotton South*, 1978.

Section Two

"The Peculiar Institution: Slavery as It Was Perceived and as It Was"

From Chapter 19 of *The American Past: A Survey of American History*

Pages 363-379

19
CHAPTER

The Peculiar Institution

Slavery as It Was Perceived and as It Was

Oppression has, at one stroke, deprived the descendants of the Africans of almost all the privileges of humanity. The Negro of the United States has lost all remembrance of his country; the language which his forefathers spoke is never heard around him; he abjured their religion and forgot their customs when he ceased to belong to Africa, without acquiring any European privileges. But he remains halfway between the two communities; sold by the one, repulsed by the other; finding not a spot in the universe to call by the name of country, except the faint image of a home which the shelter of his master's roof affords.

—*Alexis de Tocqueville*

O how accursed is that system, which entombs the godlike mind of man, defaces the divine image, reduces those who by creation were crowned with glory and honor to a level with four-footed beasts, and exalts the dealer in human flesh above all that is called God!

—*William Lloyd Garrison*

In December 1865, the Thirteenth Amendment to the Constitution was ratified and became a part of the basic law of the land. It is one of the shortest amendments, but in terms of what it did, it was the most momentous. In providing that "neither slavery nor involuntary servitude . . . shall exist within the United States," the Thirteenth wrote an end to the "great exception," a legal and social institution that flew in the face of the ideals that Americans believed gave their nation special meaning to the world, and to which they have been generally devoted: the freedom of the individual, impartial justice, equality of opportunity, and government by the people.

IMAGES OF SLAVERY

Since 1865, two images of slavery, one oozing romance, the other rife with horrors, have competed for possession of the American memory. Both visions actually took shape before 1865, when slavery was still a living institution. The seeds of the former were planted by the positive-good theorists with the assistance of a Pennsylvania-born songwriter who spent only a few months of his life in the South. The latter was cultivated in abundant detail by northern abolitionists who also, with the exception of a few African American activists, had little firsthand knowledge of the slave states.

Stephen Foster and the Sweet Magnolia

Stephen Foster was born in Pittsburgh in 1826. Musically inclined from youth, he was a pioneer of "pop music," one of the first Americans to support himself by composing songs that captured the fancy of a mass market. He wrote for traveling minstrel shows and sold sheet music, the songwriter's chief commodity before the invention of the player piano and the phonograph.

Foster's first successful song was "Oh! Susannah," a whimsical nonsense piece about the California gold rush of 1849 that is still popular in elementary school sing-alongs. Then, perhaps because the minstrel show was set in the South, with white (and sometimes black) performers rubbing burnt cork on their faces and joshing and singing in grotesquely exaggerated African American dialect, Foster turned to sentimental depictions of plantation life, often from the slave's perspective. In the world of "Swanee River" (1851), "Massa's in de Cold, Cold Ground" (1852), "My Old Kentucky Home" (1853), and "Old Black Joe" (1860), slaves were uncomplicated, loving creatures who enjoyed a simple but secure and satisfying life attached to a kindly old "Massa" who beamed kindly on his loyal "darkies."

Dancing, laughing blacks, grand houses, Spanish moss, the plunking of the banjo, the sweet scent of magnolia blossoms, and easygoing white folks were the ingredients of Foster's South, and it is well to remember that he was immensely popular in the heyday of the abolitionist movement. Within a generation of the Thirteenth Amendment, this vision of antebellum southern life was embraced by most white Americans, perhaps northerners above all. In the industrial age of the late nineteenth century—dirty, urban, and paced by the relentless drive of the machine, it was consol-

Devoted to Ol' Massa

Down in de cornfield
Hear dat mournful sound!
All de darkies am a-weeping
Massa's in de cold, cold ground.

Stephen Foster, 1852

King Cotton

Southern politicians repeatedly lectured northerners that the South supported the national economy. That is, the money that cotton brought in from abroad provided most of the surplus capital that paid for the industrialization of the nation. This transaction was direct when protective tariffs on English-made goods forced southerners to buy American-made goods.

The politicians were right. Cotton did industrialize the United States before the Civil War. However, northern antislavery people had another way of considering this economic fact of life. Who, they asked, really produced the cotton? To a large extent, slaves did. And to that extent, the United States was industrialized by the forced labor of the blacks.

This romanticized depiction of slaves by Eastman Johnson presented just the picture defenders of slavery wanted the world to see: simple, comfortable, contented slaves.

ing to dream nostalgically of a South that had never been. The tradition culminated in Margaret Mitchell's novel of 1936, *Gone with the Wind*, and Hollywood's classic film based on the book (1939).

Theodore Dwight Weld and His Converts

Abolitionists depicted rather a different slavery. To these zealous black and white lecturers, journalists, and preachers who crisscrossed the northern states, the slave's world was a bawling hell of blacksnake whips, brutal slave catchers following packs of bloodhounds, children torn from their mothers' breasts to be sold down the river, squalor, disease, and near starvation under callous, arrogant masters, the sinister slavocrats.

William Lloyd Garrison was far from alone in presenting this message to northerners. Indeed, because of his rasping self-righteousness, he was probably less effective in the attack on slavery than people like Theodore Dwight Weld, a white evangelist, "as eloquent as an angel and powerful as thunder." Weld concentrated on converting prominent people to the antislavery cause. Two of his proselytes, Arthur and Lewis Tappan, were wealthy New York merchants who generously financed abolitionist institutions like Garrison's *Liberator*, Kenyon and Oberlin Colleges in Ohio, and the American Anti-Slavery Society, founded in 1833.

Another Weld convert was James G. Birney, an Alabama planter who freed his slaves and ran as the presidential candidate of the antislavery Liberty party in 1840 and 1844. Weld married yet another abolitionist

Most slaves were used as field hands and performed the heavy labor needed to raise such cash crops as cotton.

who had owned slaves, Angelina Grimké of a prominent South Carolina family. She and her sister Sarah instilled in him a perspective on the problem of slavery that was forever beyond Garrison, a consideration for the moral plight of the conscientious slave owner.

A Strange Species of Property

The slave's status as personal property worked only one way. That is, while the slave owner's rights over his slave were much the same as his rights over his cattle, slaves did not benefit from the exemptions other personal property enjoyed in the law. A cow, a hog, or a share of stock cannot commit a crime and be punished for doing so. Slaves could and, of course, were.

Black Abolitionists

While the abolitionist movement attracted white people, it was, unsurprisingly, most dependably supported by the free blacks of the North. Although generally poor, blacks provided a disproportionate share of the money needed to publish antislavery newspapers and send antislavery lecturers. Several prominent abolitionist crusaders were black.

Sojourner Truth was the name taken by a physical giant of a woman born as the slave Isabella in New York in 1797. Freed under the state emancipation law of 1827, she worked as a domestic servant for several years and then burst onto the abolitionist scene as one of the movement's most powerful orators. Sojourner Truth was illiterate to the end of her days—she died in 1893, at 96 years of age—but she transfixed audiences when she accompanied her speeches with songs she had written herself.

Sojourner Truth (ca. 1797–1883) was a freed slave who devoted herself to the abolition and women's rights movements.

The most compelling of the black abolitionist orators was Frederick Douglass, who was born a slave in Maryland in 1817. Escaping to Massachusetts, he educated himself and, in 1845, wrote his autobiography, which, until the publication of *Uncle Tom's Cabin* in 1851 and 1852, was the most widely read antislavery document. Unlike most white abolitionists, Douglass could speak firsthand of life in a slave society and his message was no less troubling. For a while, because his former master was pursuing him, Douglass lived in England, where he furthered his education while friends back home purchased his freedom.

Harriet Beecher Stowe

The decisive antislavery argument was that it reduced human beings to the status of livestock, mere property. However, rather than dwell on a point that seemed abstract to many people, black and white abolitionists alike focused on the physical deprivations and cruelties suffered by slaves. Some antislavery lecturers traveled with runaway slaves whose backs had been disfigured from brutal beatings.

The loudest single shot in this campaign was *Uncle Tom's Cabin, or Life among the Lowly*, written by Harriet Beecher Stowe, the daughter of Lyman Beecher, the Presbyterian minister who spearheaded the anti-Catholic agitations of the 1830s. Not only did Stowe's book sell an astonishing 3,000 copies the day it was published, and 300,000 copies within a year (roughly the equivalent of 3 million copies today), but it was adapted into a play that was performed by dozens of professional and amateur troupes in small towns and cities alike. So influential was Mrs. Stowe's tale of Uncle Tom, a submissive and loyal old slave, that when Abraham Lincoln was introduced to her during the Civil War, he is said to have remarked, "So you are the little woman who wrote the book that made this great war."

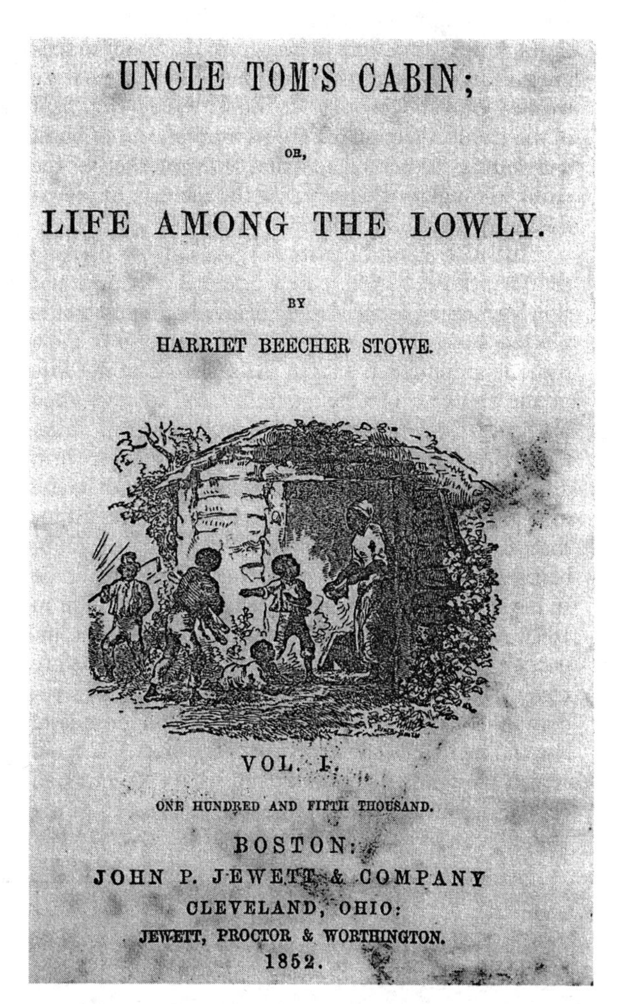

UNCLE TOM'S CABIN;

OR,

LIFE AMONG THE LOWLY.

BY

HARRIET BEECHER STOWE.

VOL. I.

ONE HUNDRED AND FIFTH THOUSAND.

BOSTON:
JOHN P. JEWETT & COMPANY
CLEVELAND, OHIO:
JEWETT, PROCTOR & WORTHINGTON.
1852.

First published as a serial in 1851 and 1852, the book version of Uncle Tom's Cabin *was widely read, selling 300,000 copies within a year.*

Notable People

Frederick Douglass

Frederick Douglass was born in Talbot County, Maryland, about 1817. He did not know the actual day of his birth because he was born a slave. "By far the larger part of slaves," Douglass wrote, "know as little of their ages as horses know of theirs, and it is the wish of most masters within my knowledge to keep their slaves thus ignorant." Douglass met his mother, Harriett Bailey, only a few times. It was the custom in his part of the South to separate children from their mother when they were weaned, probably in order "to hinder the development of the child's affection toward its mother, and to blunt and destroy the natural affection of the mother for the child." Douglass did not know the identity of his father, only that he was white.

In 1838, about 21 years of age, Douglass escaped to Massachusetts, where he worked as a laborer and slowly emerged as the leading black abolitionist in the United States. He was both a stentorian orator and a superb pamphleteer. Taught the alphabet by the wife of one of his owners, he taught himself to read when his benefactress was ordered to stop educating him. His writing style was concrete and straightforward, devoid of the flowery extravagance favored in the mid-nineteenth century and all the more forceful for that. Indeed, when critics said Douglass lied about being a slave because no self-educated man could be so eloquent, he published a *Narrative* of his life in 1845. Although the book became the single most important document of the antislavery movement before *Uncle Tom's Cabin*, its publication put Douglass's freedom in jeopardy. He was still a fugitive under federal law and he named the names of his owners. To avoid arrest, Douglass fled to England where he amassed enough money to buy his freedom and return to the United States.

For the rest of his life, as orator, politician, editor, and author, Douglass was in the forefront of the American reform. Opposition to slavery preoccupied him until the Civil War. Then he turned his attention to civil rights for blacks, women's suffrage, and the cause of factory workers. With a Republican in the White House during most of the final 30 years of his life, he enjoyed the security of federal office, culminating in his appointment as minister to Haiti in 1889.

Douglass's importance to the antislavery movement rests in the fact that his intelligence and profound personal dignity had survived the degradations of slavery. His existence gave the lie to the proslavery argument that black people were racially incapable of citizenship. Moreover, while his personal experience of slavery included many horrors, which he did not hesitate to relate in lurid detail, Douglass emphasized the fact that the evil of slavery depended not on how slaves were actually treated, but lay in the nature of the institution. His theme was the dehumanization of both slave owner and slave. There has not been an indictment of slavery written since Douglass which cannot be found, usually well-developed, in his numerous writings.

He was as passionate an abolitionist as his white friend, William Lloyd Garrison, but far more humane a man. His hatred of slavery and other injustice was almost always accompanied by an attempt to understand those responsible for the institution. There was no racism in Frederick Douglass, which could not be said of others in the reform movement. When, in 1884, Douglass married a second time, to a white woman, many old abolitionist colleagues criticized him. Douglass shrugged with splendid insouciance that he was impartial: his first wife "was the color of my mother, and the second, the color of my father." He was the first in the line of the great spokesmen for African Americans that includes Booker T. Washington, Martin Luther King, Jr., and Malcolm X.

As a work of literature, *Uncle Tom's Cabin* is deficient, but its underlying theme is subtle: no matter how decent and well-intentioned the individual slave owner, he cannot help but do wrong by living with an inherently evil institution. In the story, Uncle Tom's original owner is the epitome of the paternalistic planter who genuinely loves his old slave—the proslavery argument's beau idéal. Nevertheless, when financial troubles make it necessary for him to raise money quickly, he is forced to sell his Tom. Heartbroken, the planter promises Tom that he will find him and buy him back as soon as he is able. Nevertheless, *he sells his beloved friend because he can; the law makes Tom a commodity!*

It was not, however, this insight into the peculiar institution that made *Uncle Tom's Cabin* so popular. Rather, the book's effectiveness owed to its graphic, lurid scenes of cruelty that Tom witnesses and suffers in the course of the story. Mrs. Stowe herself accepted this as the book's contribution. When southerners angrily complained that she had distorted the realities of slave life, she responded in 1853 with *A Key to Uncle Tom's Cabin*, which set out the documentary basis of most of her accusations, much of it quotations from southern newspapers.

Blacks never forgot this side of slavery, but with the ascendancy of the romantic version in the late nineteenth century, most white Americans did. Not until the civil rights movement of the 1950s and 1960s awakened the country to the tragic history of American blacks did the ugly face of the peculiar institution again impress itself on the popular consciousness.

WHAT SLAVERY WAS LIKE

Which image is correct? Both and neither. Although proslavery and antislavery partisans dealt with the peculiar institution as though it were monolithic, the same thing in Virginia and Texas, on cotton plantation and New Orleans river front, on sprawling plantation and gloomy frontier homestead, for field hand and big house butler, the reality of slavery was as diverse as the South itself.

Structure of the Institution: White Perspective

The census of 1860, the last census that was taken while slavery was legal, revealed that nearly 4 million people lived in bondage. They were equally divided between males and females. All but a handful lived in the 15 states south of the Mason-Dixon line and the Ohio River. West of the Mississippi River, Missouri, Arkansas, Louisiana, and Texas were slave states.

Only one white southern family in four owned slaves. Even when those whose living depended directly on the existence of the institution—overseers, slave traders, and patrollers—are added in, it is clear that only a minority of white southerners had a material stake in slavery.

Those who were very rich and politically powerful because they owned slaves were particularly few. In 1860, only 2,200 great planters, less than 1 percent of the southern population, owned 100 or more slaves. Only 254 persons owned 200 or more. Nathaniel Heyward of South Carolina was at the top of this dubious pyramid; he owned 2,000 slaves on 17 plantations.

More typical of the southern slave owner was Jacob Eaton of neighboring North Carolina. On his 160-acre farm he worked side by side with the slave family he owned. Eaton's yeoman class—small independent farmers who owned one to nine slaves—was the backbone of both the South and the slavery system. About 74 percent of southern slave owners fell into this category. Another 16 percent of slave owners fell into the middle category of those who owned between 10 and 20 people. A mere 10 percent of slave owners owned more than 20 slaves.

Structure of the Institution: Black Perspective

If the big plantation was rare from a white perspective, life in the shadow of the big house was more common in the eyes of the blacks. By 1860, more than half the slaves lived on what we would think of as a plantation rather than a farm. Perhaps half a million belonged to members of the great planter class.

There were a few black slave owners. The census of 1830 revealed 3,775 free African Americans in possession of 12,760 black slaves. One of the most bizarre cases was that of Dilsey Pope, a free black woman of Columbus, Georgia, who owned her husband. There was a fierce quarrel and Mrs. Pope sold him to a white neighbor. When the couple reconciled, the new owner refused to sell the husband back to Mrs. Pope. (Their marriage had no standing in the law.)

There were even some great planters who were black. Andrew Durnford of New Orleans owned 77 slaves. When questioned about this, Durnford said frankly that his ownership of other blacks was self-interest. Owning slaves was the way to wealth in the South. Although he contributed to the American Colonization Society, Durnford freed only four slaves during his lifetime, another in his will.

First Light to Sundown

Few blacks enjoyed the material advantages of living—better food, clothing, sanitation, sometimes living quarters—as domestic servants. Cooks, maids, butlers, valets, and footmen made life more pleasant

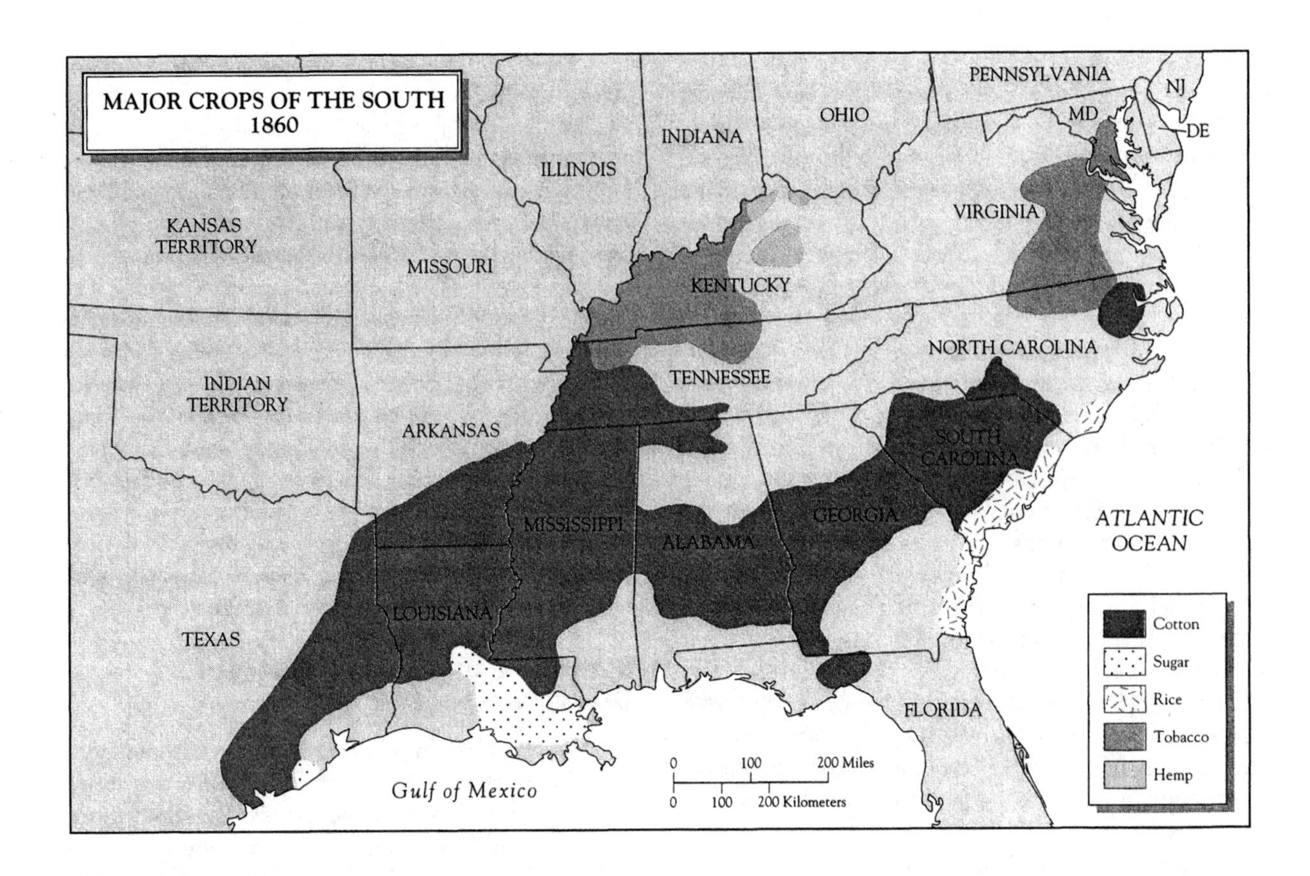

for the great planters who could afford them, but they did not make money for their masters. The vast majority of slaves were field hands who raised a cash crop by means of heavy labor from first light to sundown almost year-round. For a slave owner to justify investing capital in a labor force rather than hiring free laborers and putting his capital elsewhere, it was necessary to keep the property hopping.

Cotton was by far the most important southern product (the most important *American* product!). During the 1850s, an average annual crop of 4 million bales brought more than $190 million into the American economy from abroad. Cotton represented two-thirds of the nation's total exports and (in 1850) fully 1.8 million slaves out of 3.2 million worked it. Other cash crops that slaves raised were tobacco (350,000 slaves), sugar (150,000), rice (125,000), and hemp, from which rope was manufactured (60,000).

Southern farmers and planters strove to be self-sufficient. Therefore, slaves raised corn, vegetables, and hogs for food, and hay for fodder, as well as their cash crop. There was plenty of work to be done on farm or plantation year-round. The calendar of a cotton plantation was packed with jobs, major and odd, except for a short period around Christmas, to which the slaves looked forward as "laying-by time."

Curiously, because slaves were expensive—up to $2,000 for a first-rate field hand, a healthy man in the prime of life—planters preferred to hire free black or Irish workers to perform some unhealthy and dangerous tasks. Few risked their costly human property on draining swamps or working at the bottom of chutes down which 600-pound bales of cotton came hurtling at high speeds, sometimes flipping end over end.

The Rhythms of Labor

By the 1850s, a slave produced from $80 to $120 in value each year and cost between $30 and $50 to feed, clothe, and shelter. The margin of profit was not large enough to allow the small-scale slave owner to live without working in the fields along with his slaves.

Planters who owned 10 to 20 slaves were less likely to perform menial tasks. But because slaves rarely worked any more than they were forced to do (their share of the fruits of their labor was quite firmly fixed) the owner had to supervise them—constantly bribing, cajoling, threatening, or whipping them to

Washington the Slave Owner

At the time of his death in 1799, George Washington owned 300 slaves at Mount Vernon and four additional plantations. The father-of-his-country's record as a patriarch was mixed. On the one hand, according to a visitor from Poland, the slaves' houses at Washington's River Farm were "more miserable than the most miserable cottages of our peasants." Washington himself expressed embarrassment over living conditions at River Farm.

On the other hand, Washington was deeply concerned to respect his slaves' family and marriage relationships. Children remained with their mothers until age 14. Slave husbands and wives were separated when one but not the other was needed elsewhere, and some of Washington's slaves were married to the slaves of other planters or to free blacks. However, Washington meticulously recorded who was tied to whom, and he refused to sell costly surplus slaves "because they could not be disposed of in families . . . and to disperse the families I have an aversion."

Moreover, Washington's plantations were within four miles of one another and "nightwalking," conjugal visits, were a constant problem of which he complained but did little. In his will, Washington provided that his slaves be freed only after his wife's death because they had intermarried with Martha Washington's "Dower Negroes" and it "would excite the most painful sensations" if they were to be separated.

move along. With more than 20 slaves, a planter could afford to hire a professional overseer or to put a straw boss or slave driver (himself a slave) in charge of supervision. On the very large plantations, masters had little direct contact with their field hands. They could cultivate a genuine ignorance of how overseers and straw bosses mistreated their "people."

Slaves on larger plantations worked according to the task system or the gang system. Under the task system, a specific job was assigned each day. When it was done, the slave's time was his or her own. For some planters this was the most efficient form of organization because, when provided with an incentive, however meager, the slaves worked harder. Others complained that the result of the task system was slipshod labor as their workers rushed through their tasks to get to their own chores or recreation.

Under the gang system, slaves worked from sunrise to sundown in groups under a white overseer or black driver. It is impossible to know how frequently they felt the sting of the blacksnake. The lash was always in evidence, however, in black hand as well as white. Frederick Douglass wryly remarked that "everybody in the South wants the privilege of whipping someone else."

The Slave Trade

Slaves were defined in law as chattel property, personal movable possessions legally much the same as cattle, hogs, a cotton gin, a chair, or a share of stock. They could be bought, sold, bartered, willed, or given away as a present. In practice in the volatile cotton economy, the commerce in slaves was brisk and potentially quite profitable.

The slave trade was the ugliest face of slavery. Even strident defenders of the institution admitted it. The general flow of the commerce was down the river—the Mississippi—from the older tobacco states to the cotton states of the Deep South. Professional slave traders bought blacks in Virginia and Maryland, and shipped them or marched them in coffles (groups chained together in a line) to New Orleans, where as many as 200 companies were in the business.

The slave auction was in many ways like a livestock auction. Foreigners, northerners, and many southerners were simultaneously disgusted and fascinated by them, much as American tourists in Mexico or Spain today react to bullfights. Prospective buyers crowded around the auction block, examining the teeth of the slaves in which they were interested, as they would examine those of horses; running them around to test their wind; wiping handkerchiefs over their bodies to determine if the auctioneer had dyed gray hairs black or rubbed oil into aged dry skin; and then raucously entering their bids.

Some abolitionists claimed that slaves were methodically bred like animals. Indeed, women were rewarded for bearing children, thus increasing their owners' wealth, and were sometimes described in auction advertisements as good breeders. In Maryland, census takers discovered plantations on which the workforce consisted of one adult male, half a dozen young women, and perhaps twice that many small children—not a group likely to get a lot done if agriculture was the idea. However, the gospel of

Slaves were kept in these cells in Alexandria, Virginia, until they were sold by slave traders.

the positive-good required slave owners who took it seriously to abhor such immorality, and slave breeding as a business was undoubtedly rare.

Masters aspiring to be patriarchs disapproved of everything about the slave trade, describing slave traders as base, crude, unworthy men. Nevertheless, as Harriet Beecher Stowe and others pointed out, without the slave trade there could be no slavery. If some humans were to be property, others had to have the right to buy and sell them. Where there is trade, there must be brokers.

The Foreign Slave Trade

After 1808, it was a violation of federal law to import slaves. But when the price of slaves was high, some buccaneers were willing to try to bring in blacks from West Africa or Cuba.

It was a risky business. The Royal Navy patrolled African waters, and American naval vessels cruised the Atlantic and Gulf coasts. Nevertheless, an estimated 50,000 to 55,000 Africans and black Cubans were smuggled into the United States between 1808 and 1861. During the 1850s, several travelers in the South reported seeing a number of black men and women with filed teeth, tattoos, and ritual mutilations that were practiced only in Africa. On the very eve of the Civil War, a slave vessel successfully made its way into the Charleston harbor.

In the late 1850s, the price of slaves soared beyond the reach of all but the very wealthy. A group of southern politicians met at Vicksburg, Mississippi, and formally demanded the reopening of the African slave trade. Such a law would never have passed Congress, but the Vicksburg Convention alarmed many northerners and contributed to the hardening of sectional hostilities that contributed to the Civil War.

LIFE IN THE QUARTERS

The slave codes of most southern states provided that slaves had no civil rights. They could not own property under the law; therefore, they could not legally buy and sell anything. They could not make contracts. They could not marry legally. They could not testify in court against any white person (nor could free blacks in most southern states). They could not even leave the plantation without their owners' written permission.

It was a crime for a slave to strike a white person under any circumstances, even self-defense. Slaves could not carry firearms. They could not congregate in more than small groups except at religious services under white supervision. They could not be abroad at night. And in most southern states, it was a crime for a white or another black to teach a slave to read.

The slaves' rights were those to life and, under most slave codes, a minimum standard of food, clothing, and shelter.

Humans without Human Rights

The actual experience of slave life had little to do with the letter of the slave codes; for example, it was not accounted murder when a master killed a slave during "moderate" or "reasonable" punishment, words difficult to define in courts. Whipping was the most common means of corporal punishment, and 50 lashes—quite enough to kill a man—was not an uncommon sentence. In the end, the slaves' only guarantee against death or brutal mistreatment at the hands of their masters was the gospel of patriarchy, social pressure, public opinion, religious scruples, and the cash value of the slaves.

There are few better guarantees than a man's self-esteem and his money, but neither was foolproof. Struggling slave owners had little time for their genteel neighbors' opinions of their moral sense. Slave owners and overseers did fly into uncontrolled rages and kill slaves. Because their property rights in their slaves inevitably took precedence over the slaves' few human rights, owners were rarely punished. After an incident of hideous torture in Virginia in 1858, with the slave victim dying after 24 hours of beating and burning, the law punished the sadistic master by imprisoning him. But he was not required to forfeit ownership of several other blacks.

A Diverse Institution

If the laws protecting slaves were not effective, it was also true that many slave owners were moved by personal decency and by their determination to live up to the ideal of the benevolent patriarch to care for their slaves far better than the law required, and sometimes in violation of the slave codes.

A family that owned only one or two slaves occasionally developed a relationship much like partnership with them. White owners and black slaves ate the same food, slept in the same cabin, and worked together intimately. On the whole, however, the slave on a large plantation was more likely to be better off, simply because of the poverty of the struggling small farmer.

After about 1840, large-scale slave owners generally provided simple but adequate rations. It was common to allow slaves to keep their own vegetable plots and even chickens; masters sometimes did not keep their own gardens and coops but bought vegetables and eggs from their slaves. Here and there was a master who allowed the blacks to raise hogs for their own use, but the master could not always be sure if the pork chop on the slave's table was the slave's own or stolen from him.

Some slaves were permitted to buy and sell outside the boundaries of the plantation and to keep the money they earned. Along the Mississippi River, task system slaves working on their own time cut wood for the steamboats. Some sold chickens and eggs in nearby towns, and some slaves even kept shotguns for hunting. One remarkable character was Simon Gray, a skilled flatboatman who was paid $8 a month to haul lumber to New Orleans. Gray commanded crews of up to 20 men, including free whites, and kept detailed accounts for his owner. He eventually bought his own freedom.

A few masters permitted their slaves to save money in order to purchase their own, their spouse's, or their children's freedom. In at least one instance, a Kentucky judge actually enforced an agreement on

This photograph of an African American with instruments of punishment was widely distributed to raise money "for the benefit of colored people."

a purchase price between a master and slave as a valid contract.

Another example of open violation of the slave code was on the model plantation of Joseph Davis, brother of Jefferson Davis, the future president of the Confederate States of America. Ignoring a Mississippi state law forbidding the education of blacks, Joseph Davis maintained a school and teacher for the children of the quarters.

It is important to recall, however, that for every master like Joseph Davis there was another who kept his slaves just sound enough to work and who agreed with the man who wrote without embarrassment to a magazine that "Africans are nothing but brutes,

Freedom Song

When Israel was in Egypt land
Let my people go
Oppressed so hard they could not stand
Let my people go.
Go down, Moses,
Way down in Egypt land
Tell old Pharaoh
To let my people go.

and they will love you better for whipping, whether they deserve it or not."

MODES OF PROTEST

Whether their master was kindly or cruel, their material circumstances adequate or execrable, the blacks hated their lot in life. While some were deeply and sincerely attached to their masters, and while rebellion was rare after Nat Turner, the blacks resisted slavery in other ways. When freedom became a realistic possibility during the Civil War, slaves deserted their homes by the thousands to flee to Union lines and, in the case of the young men, to enlist in the Union Army. As a South Carolina planter wrote candidly after the war, "I believed these people were content, happy, and attached to their masters." That, he concluded sadly, was a delusion.

Malingering and Thieving

This honest man might have been spared his disappointment had he given deeper consideration to white people's stereotypes of the blacks under slavery. It was commonly held that blacks were inherently lazy, irresponsible, and would not work except under close supervision. In fact, free blacks generally worked quite hard, and the same slaves whose laziness was a constant aggravation in the cotton fields, toiled in their own gardens from dawn to dusk on Sundays and often, by moonlight, during the week. In slavery, the only incentive to work hard for the master was negative—the threat of punishment—and that incentive was often not enough to cause men and women to ignore the blazing southern sun. When the overseer or driver was over the hill, it was nap time.

Theft was so common on plantations that whites believed blacks to be congenital thieves. Again, the only incentive not to steal a chicken, a suckling pig, or a berry pie from the big-house kitchen was fear of punishment. If a slave was not caught, he had no reason to believe he had done wrong. One chicken thief who was caught in the act of eating his prize explained this point trenchantly to his master: if the chicken was master's property and he was master's property, then master had not lost anything because the chicken was in his belly instead of scratching around the hen yard. It is not known if this meditation saved the philosopher from a whipping.

Running Away

The most direct testimony of slave discontent was the prevalence of runaways. Only blacks who lived in the states that bordered the free states—Delaware, Maryland, Kentucky—had a reasonable chance of escaping

Uncle Remus Explains

Many historians of slavery believe that because violent resistance by blacks was suicidal, many slaves (and post–Civil War southern blacks) devised the technique of "playing Uncle Tom," that is, playing a docile role in front of whites in order to survive. Uncle Remus describes this behavior in "Why Br'er Possum Loves Peace." Mr. Dog attacks Br'er Coon and Br'er Possum. Br'er Coon fights back and drives Mr. Dog away, but at the price of taking some damage himself. In the meantime, Br'er Possum plays possum, plays dead.

Later, representing blacks who want to fight back, Br'er Coon berates Br'er Possum for cowardice. "'I ain't runnin' wid cowards deze days,' sez Br'er Coon." Br'er Possum replies that just because he did not fight does not mean that he is a coward:

> *I want no mo' skeer'd dan you is right now . . . but I'm de most ticklish chap w'at you ever laid eyes on, en no sooner did Mr. Dog put his nose down yer 'mong my ribs dan I got ter laffin. . . . I don't mine fightin', Br'er Coon, no mo' dan you duz . . . but I declar' ter grashus ef I kin stan' ticklin.*

Wit, not violence, was the way to deal with vicious whites. Note that it is Mr. Dog, not Br'er—Brother.

to permanent freedom. A great many were successful "riding" what they called the "underground railway," rushing at night from hiding places in one abolitionist's home to another. Because the railway was not so well organized as legend has it, most runaways who succeeded probably did so on their own devices, or by depending on African American "conductors." Harriet Tubman, who escaped from her master in 1849, returned to the South 19 times to lead other blacks to freedom. (During the Civil War, Tubman was a Union spy behind Confederate lines.)

In calling for a stricter Fugitive Slave Act in 1850 (a law that gave the federal government the responsibility of returning slaves), southerners estimated that as many as 100,000 blacks escaped to the free states. Several times that number tried and failed.

Common throughout the South was running away in the full knowledge that capture and punishment were inevitable. Nevertheless, the appeal of a few days or weeks of freedom, or the chance to visit a spouse or a friend on another plantation, was worth the risk to so many blacks that runaway slaves were a vexation to masters from Maryland to Mississippi.

Runaways in hiding relied on other blacks to conceal and feed them. The fact that they were hidden and fed at risk to their benefactors of corporal punishment reveals the existence of a sense of solidarity among the slaves that can never be fully understood by historians because the slaves kept no written records. But some indication of the quality of life in the slave quarters from sundown to first light can be conjectured from what is known of black religion and folklore.

Let My People Go

By the 1850s, most slaves had warmly embraced an emotional brand of Protestant Christianity that was basically Baptist and Methodist in temper. Religious services were replete with animated sermons by unlettered but charismatic preachers and exuberant rhythmic singing, the Negro spirituals loved by whites as well as by blacks.

In the sermons and spirituals, hymns that combined biblical themes with African musical forms, the slaves explicitly identified with the ancient Hebrews. While in bondage in Babylon and Egypt, the Hebrews had been, in their simplicity and poverty, God's chosen people. In the afterlife, all human beings would be equal and happy.

Harriet Tubman (left; ca. 1820–1913) stands with a group of slaves she helped escape to freedom.

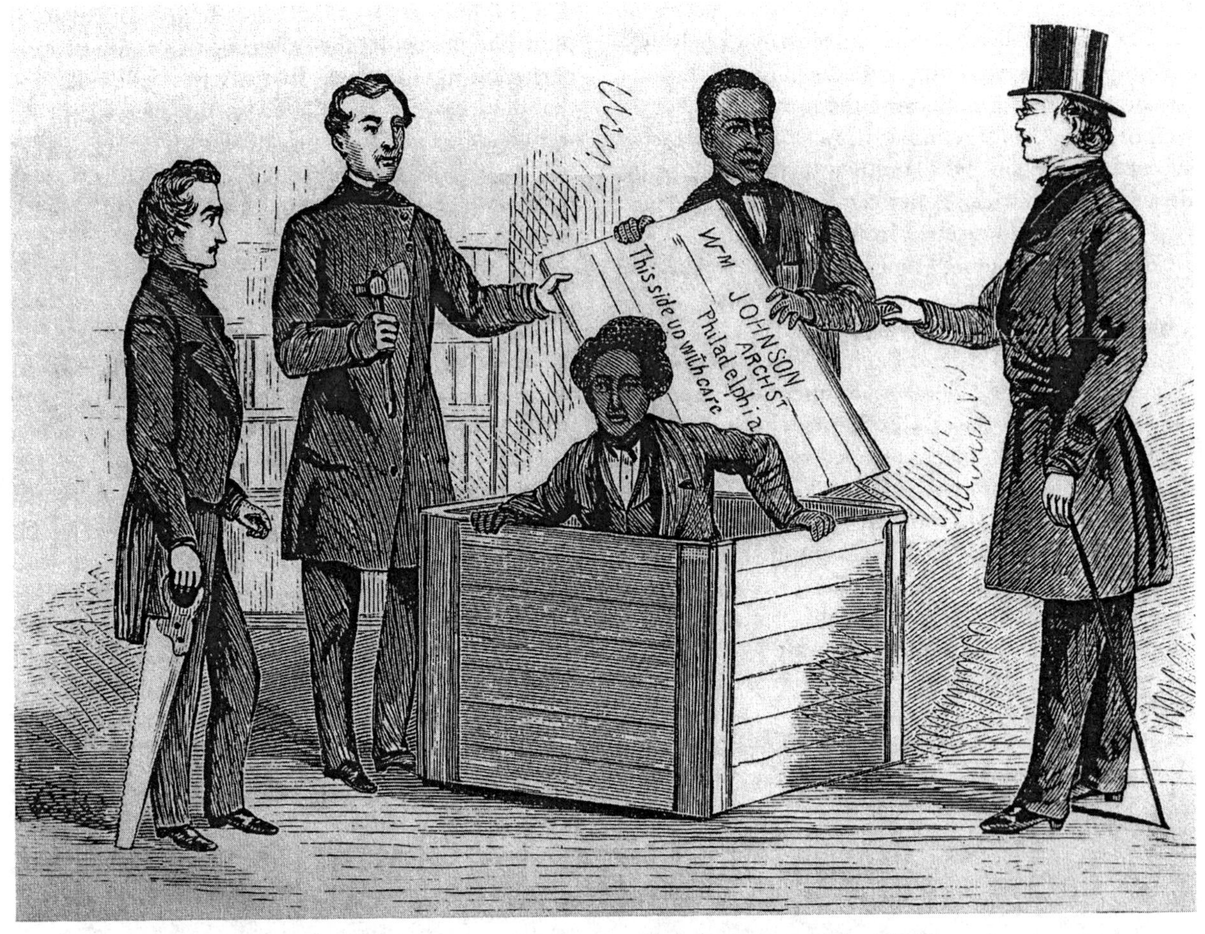

Henry Brown's escape from slavery in a shipping crate earned him the nickname "Box" for the remainder of his life.

This cry of protest was not lost on the whites. But as long as they believed that slaves associated freedom with the next life, there was no reason to stifle the cry. However, there was also a worldly facet of slave religion. Biblical characters who were delivered in life, such as Joshua, Jonah, and Daniel, were heroes in African American hagiography. One kind of spiritual, such as "Ride on, King Jesus," depicted Christ as a warrior messiah. The implications were obvious.

"Bred en Bawn in a Brier-Patch"

Another thinly masked form of protest was the folk tales for which black storytellers became famous, particularly the Br'er Rabbit stories that were collected after the Civil War as *Uncle Remus: His Songs and Sayings* by Georgia journalist Joel Chandler Harris. In these yarns, elements of which have been traced back to West African folklore, the rabbit, a weak victim of stronger animals and unable to defend himself by force, survives and flourishes through the use of trickery and complex deceits.

In the most famous of the Uncle Remus stories, "How Mr. Rabbit Was Too Sharp for Mr. Fox," Br'er Fox has the rabbit in his hands and is debating with himself whether to barbecue him, hang him, drown him, or skin him. Br'er Rabbit assures the fox that he will be happy with any of these fates as long as the fox does not fling him into a nearby brier-patch, which he fears more than anything. Of course, that is exactly what Br'er Fox does, whence Br'er Rabbit is home free. "Bred en bawn in a brier-patch, Br'er Fox," Br'er Rabbit shouts back tauntingly, "bred en bawn in a brier-patch." The slaves, unable to taunt their masters so bluntly, satisfied themselves with quiet trickery and coded tales about it.

It is worth noting that in the Uncle Remus stories, Br'er Rabbit now and then outsmarts himself and suffers for it. As in all social commentary of substance, the slaves were as sensitive to their own foibles as to those of their masters.

The Slave Community

Like Br'er Rabbit, slaves presented a different face to whites than among their own people. Often, individuals reinforced white beliefs in their inferiority by playing the lazy, dimwitted, comical "Sambo," quite devoted to "Ol' Marse" and patently incapable of taking care of themselves. Some observant whites noticed that Sambo was quick-witted enough when surprised while talking to other slaves, or that he literally slaved in his own garden and only slept in the cotton fields.

For the most part, however, the vitality of black culture and the slave community remained concealed from whites. It can be read only in the folktales and sermons and recollections of slavery gathered after emancipation. Perhaps the most striking demonstration of the resourcefulness of the blacks in sticking together for mutual support lies in the fact that family connections were powerful and productive. By 1865, when slavery was abolished, there were ten times as many slaves in the United States as had been imported from Africa and the West Indies. The American slave population was the only one in the Western Hemisphere to increase as a result of natural reproduction. Only after the blacks of South and Central America were freed from bondage did their numbers grow naturally.

Against all odds, the nuclear family was a strong institution among slaves and remained so after emancipation, as this photo of Virginia peanut farmers implies.

CHRONOLOGY

1818	African slave trade abolished
1851–1860	Stephen Foster's sentimental songs of an idyllic South are published
1840, 1844	James G. Birney is presidential candidate for abolitionist Liberty party
1845	Publication of Frederick Douglass's Autobiography
1850	Strict and effective Fugitive Slave Law enacted Slave trade abolished in Washington
1851	Publication of Harriet Beecher Stowe's *Uncle Tom's Cabin*
1936	Publication of Margaret Mitchell's *Gone with the Wind* (film in 1939)

FOR FURTHER READING

Ulrich B. Phillips, *American Negro Slavery*, 1919, and *Life and Labor in the Old South*, 1929, present sometimes romanticized, almost sympathetic portraits of slavery, and yet, despite the bias of the books, they contain much valuable information and are congenially written. Kenneth Stampp, *The Peculiar Institution*, 1956, was an explicit response to Phillips and is equally valuable.

Since the 1960s, slavery has been studied exhaustively in virtually all its aspects. Just a few of the hundreds of titles include Ira Berlin, *Slaves without Masters*, 1975; John Blassingame, *The Slave Community*, 1972, and *Slave Testimony*, 1977; Carl N. Degler, *Neither Black nor White: Slavery and Race Relations in Brazil and the United States*, 1971; Stanley Elkins, *Slavery*, 1968; Robert Fogel and Stanley Engermann, *Time on the Cross*, 1974—the findings of which are attacked in Herbert Gutman and Richard Sutch, *Slavery and the Numbers Game*, 1975; Paul A. David, et al., *Reckoning with Slavery*, 1976; and Michael Tadman, *Speculators and Slaves: Traders and Slaves in the Old South*, 1989.

See also George M. Frederickson, *The Black Image in the White Mind*, 1971; Eugene Genovese, *The Political Economy of Slavery*, 1962, and *Roll Jordan Roll*, 1975; Herbert G. Gutman, *The Black Family in Slavery and Freedom, 1750–1925*, 1976; Lawrence W. Levine, *Black Culture and Black Consciousness: Afro-American Folk Thought from Slavery to Freedom*, 1977; Gilbert Osofsky, *Puttin' on Ol' Massa*, 1969; Harold Rawick, *From Sundown to Sunup*, 1967; Robert Starobin, *Industrial Slavery in the Old South*, 1970; Stephen B. Oates, *The Fires of Jubilee: Nat Turner's Fierce Rebellion*, 1975; and Jacqueline Jones, *Labor of Love, Labor of Sorrow: Black Women, Work, and the Family from Slavery to the Present*, 1985.

Useful books on abolitionism include Ronald Abzug, *Passionate Liberator: Theodore Dwight Weld and the Dilemma of Reform*, 1980; William McFeely, *Frederick Douglass*, 1991; M. L. Dillon, *The Abolitionists: The Growth of a Dissenting Minority*, 1974; Aileen S. Kraditor, *Means and Ends in American Abolitionism: Garrison and His Critics on Strategy and Tactics, 1834–50*, 1967; Gerda Lerner, *The Grimké Sisters from South Carolina: Rebels against Slavery*, 1967; Jean Fagan Yellin, *Women and Sisters: The Antislavery Feminists in American Culture*, 1989; Walter M. Merrill, *Against Wind and Tide: A Biography of William Lloyd Garrison*, 1963; Benjamin Quarles, *Black Abolitionists*, 1969; Gerald Sorin, *Abolitionism: A New Perspective*, 1972; J. B. Stewart, *Holy Warriors: The Abolitionists and American Slavery*, 1976; and B. P. Thomas, *Theodore Dwight Weld: Crusader for Freedom*, 1950.

On the pro-slavery argument, see George M. Frederickson, *The Black Image in the White Mind*, 1971; W. S. Jenkins, *Pro-Slavery Thought in the Old South*, 1935; William Stanton, *The Leopard's Spots: Scientific Attitudes toward Race in America, 1815–1859*, 1960; and Harvey Wish, *George Fitzhugh: Propagandist of the Old South*, 1943.

Section Three

"Blacks, Whites, and the Promise of a New South"

From Chapter 7 of *American Ways: A Brief History of American Culture*

Pages 175-180

BLACKS, WHITES, AND THE PROMISE OF A NEW SOUTH

As with immigrants, when Henry Seidel Canby composed his memoirs of his boyhood in Wilmington, Delaware, in the 1890s, he easily located the position of African Americans on the nation's social and cultural spectrum. African Americans were on the fringe; they were social and cultural outsiders. Regardless of their educational attainments, wealth, religious persuasion, or place of residence, skin pigmentation automatically excluded them from becoming full-scale participants in the dominant culture.

Locating the position of white southerners posed a more difficult problem for Canby and for others. In some respects white southerners seemed even more Victorian than middle-class Protestant northerners. The South was, after all, "the habitat of the quintessential WASP [white Anglo-Saxon Protestant]," Professor George B. Tindall told the Southern Historical Convention in 1973. "Is it not, in fact," he rhetorically asked, "the biggest single WASP nest this side of the Atlantic?" The great multitude of immigrants who arrived in the nineteenth and early twentieth centuries deliberately bypassed the South. Hence, the southern white population remained overwhelmingly English, Welsh, Scots, and Scots-Irish in its ethnic origins. Neither did any other region of the country approximate the South's loyalty to and enthusiasm for evangelical Protestantism. Nothing was more central to both white and black southern ways than the "old time religion," a faith based upon a literal reading of the Bible and belief in the experience of a spiritual rebirth (the conversion experience). With respect to ethnicity and religion, then, the white South qualified for full membership in the dominant Victorian culture.

Yet southern ways were not identical with those of the northern middle class. In the South, the ways of traditional hierarchy lingered on with far more force than they did in the North. Despite the enthusiasm and broad claims made on behalf of the achievements of a new, industrial South in the late nineteenth and early twentieth centuries, the full impact of the Industrial Revolution, with its large cities and sprawling middle class, failed to reach the region until the middle decades of the twentieth century. In the South, "there is in substance no middle class," said a Republican Congressman with only slight exaggeration in the 1850s. "Great wealth and hopeless poverty is the settled condition [of the region]." The long-term absence of a substantial middle class precluded the possibility of the South replicating northern ways. So did race. Unlike the North, the South was a manifestly biracial society. "Southern whites cannot walk, talk, sing, conceive of laws or justice, think of sex, love, the family or freedom without responding to the presence of Negroes," explained black novelist Ralph Ellison in 1964.

The Ways of the Newly Freed People

The Civil War and Reconstruction (1861–77) seemed to present unprecedented opportunities for radically altering southern ways. Initially, President Abraham Lincoln limited northern war aims to the restoration of the Union. But, as the war dragged on, pressures mounted for broadening the conflict's objectives. One pressure arose from African Americans; they refused to act like slaves and called the attention of northern whites to the war's revolutionary potential. The other pressure arose from northern whites, many of whom eventually came to see the war as a splendid opportunity for remaking the South in the image of the North.

The Radical Republicans, as the northern reformers were dubbed, embraced a set of divergent, but overlapping goals. As products of the antebellum abolitionist crusade, some Radicals wanted to create a far more egalitarian society, one in which skin color would count for nothing. Others cared little or nothing for the fate of blacks but hated the haughty southern white "aristocracy." Despite their differences, the Radicals eventually settled on one principal goal—the extension of equal political and civil rights to African Americans.

Given the racial attitudes of the day, this was no small step. The Thirteenth through the Fifteenth Amendments to the Constitution freed blacks from slavery, made them United States citizens, and extended suffrage to black males. The second clause of the Fourteenth Amendment prohibited the individual states from depriving any citizen of his or her rights and privileges without due process of law. This clause eventually served as the text for a far-reaching body of rights, such as the 1954 Supreme Court decision that ended the racial segregation of the nation's schools.

But Congress rejected the more extreme proposals of the Radicals. While blacks were in principle to enjoy all of the same rights as white citizens of the United States, in the end the national government was unable or unwilling to establish effective tools for securing this lofty ideal. In particular, the government failed to provide the newly freed people with the economic strength required to realize fully their rights as citizens. There was no large-scale confiscation and redistribution of southern lands, no massive federal financial assistance to the ex-slaves, nor were there provisions for extended federal protection of the freed people in the ex-Confederate states. In short, there was nothing comparable to a Marshall Plan (America's economic assistance program for Europe after World War II) for the South. A rumor spread across the South that every former slave family would receive forty acres and a mule, but nothing came of the idea. Even though white southerners had engaged in treason during the war, northerners were reluctant to take away their property (other than their property in slaves). They considered private property to be an inviolable right.

The congressional majority apparently agreed with the self-help philosophy of black leader Frederick Douglass, who in 1862 had said: "Let them [the freed people] alone. Our duty is done better by not hindering than by helping our fellow man." He added that "the best way to help them is just to let them help themselves." Equal legal rights and the right to compete unimpeded in the marketplace—these, the Radicals concluded, were enough aid to the newly freed slaves. With these rights, they thought, the freed people had the same opportunities as ordinary white families in the North. Applying the white middle-class formula of success to the newly freed blacks, they reasoned that by practicing hard work, individual initiative, and frugality the ex-slaves too could achieve economic self-sufficiency.

Realizing such an idyllic scenario turned out to be far more difficult than the northern Radicals had presumed. Apart from confronting pervasive racial prejudice and discrimination, the propertyless freed people possessed only one economic resource—their labor. Whites owned nearly all of the land, the draft animals, and the tools needed for survival. Despite these handicaps, about one-fifth of the freed families eventually obtained land of their own. But the overwhelming majority of the remainder became sharecroppers, a system that until the middle of the twentieth century came to dominate the southern countryside for both poor whites and blacks. While rarely able to improve their living standards above the subsistence level, by eliminating hated white overseers, detailed white supervision, and gang labor, the black families did enjoy in the sharecropping system more personal autonomy than they had had during slavery.

Blacks quickly seized upon their new opportunities for political participation. While underrepresented as elected officials (in terms of their proportion of the total population), during the last half of the nineteenth century hundreds of former slaves won election to public offices. Eighteen even obtained seats in the United States Congress. On the state level, blacks and their white allies (contemptuously referred to by their opponents as carpetbaggers and scalawags) established public school systems where none had existed before, drew up more humanitarian legal codes, and passed a body of civil rights legislation.

Blacks sought to make the most of their new freedom in other respects. They at once set about distancing themselves as much as they could from older forms of coercion and personal dependency. Insisting that their families should no longer act like slaves, they moved out of the former slave quarters and pulled their wives and children out of the fields. Anchored in the ways that had sustained them during slavery, the newly emancipated slaves quickly began rebuilding their own black communities. At the center of the new communities was the family. Once the war had ended in 1865, separated husbands, wives, parents, and children rushed to seek each other out and to restore severed relationships. Thousands of former slaves reaffirmed their commitments to their families by insisting on official wedding ceremonies. That black parents everywhere enthusiastically embraced opportunities for their children to learn how to read and write reflected an equal dedication to family welfare.

An African Methodist Episcopal Church in the South. Simple structures, such as this one built in the late nineteenth century, served as churches for the newly freed African American people. Along with families, churches were key institutions in perpetuating a distinctively African American culture.

Even more than in the past, religion provided a key pillar of black communities. Everywhere across the South newly freed blacks seceded from white churches and formed their own churches with their own ministers. While sharing with white evangelicals an emphasis on spiritual rebirth, black Methodist and Baptist ministers made Christianity into a religion of liberation. No themes for sermons and Sunday school lessons were more popular than Moses leading his oppressed people out of the land of bondage and of Jesus promising relief from earthly burdens. Congregational participation in worship services included exuberant expressions of religious feelings. Congregations shouted responses to calls by their preachers, they clapped their hands, and swayed in unison as they sang moving spirituals.

Preserving and Constructing a Southern Cultural Identity

Despite Reconstruction and the efforts of freed blacks to invent and perpetuate new ways, within three decades after the Civil War most blacks and perhaps many whites must have wondered if southern ways had changed very much. The much vaunted New South, which promised to bring industry, rapid economic growth, and a large middle class to the region, never achieved anything approximating full realization. True, by 1900 the South could boast of significant growth in railroad mileage, iron and steel production, timber and tobacco processing, and in textile manufacturing, but still the growth of the South's economy lagged far behind the North's. Indeed, in terms of per capita income, the region fell even further behind the North.

Neither did the destruction of slavery and plantation agriculture bring down the region's hierarchical social order. By controlling a highly disproportionate share of the South's farmlands, the families of the pre–Civil War planters retained most of their traditional economic power. In the meantime, the conditions of the yeoman white farmers deteriorated. Faced with falling cotton prices, some 80 percent of them lost their land in the postwar era.

Aiding and abetting the white South's resistance to cultural change was the invention and perpetuation of powerful myths. One was that of the Old South. In the minds of white southerners, the pre–Civil War plantation South became everything the industrial North was not. Rather than a region of smokestacks, crowded tenements, and screeching machinery, in the imaginations of both northerners and southerners the romanticized Old South evoked images of gallant gentlemen, refined ladies, contented slaves, moonlight, mint juleps, and magnolias. The Old South possessed a way of life that was less material, less hurried, and richer in the possibilities of sensual fulfillment than that of the North.

A second myth was that of the Lost Cause. It told of how brave Confederate soldiers had defended a noble way of life—the Old South—against the rapacious Yankees. Following the leadership of the United Confederate Veterans and the United Daughters of the Confederacy, between about the 1880s and the 1920s, towns across the South erected literally hundreds of monuments with statues of solitary but ever vigilant Confederate soldiers always peering northward. While southern Protestantism was sparse on iconography, the myth of the Lost Cause was another matter. It became in the words of historian Charles Reagan Wilson "a civil religion." White southerners transformed Robert E. Lee, Jefferson Davis, and other wartime heroes into saints and martyrs. For generations, Decoration Day was a special time of regional unity. Decoration Day brought out thousands of people who carried spring flowers to the graves of those who had been killed decades earlier.

Religion also bolstered the South's cultural identity. While northern Protestants were relaxing their insistence on the need for dramatic conversion experiences and on biblical literalism, southern Protestants remained loyal to their evangelical roots. "The South is by a long way the most simply and sincerely religious country that I ever was in," wrote Sir William Archer, an English visitor in 1910. For southerners, he added, "God is very real and personal." Indeed, he was. Religious faith and language extended everywhere; it permeated public discourse, courtship, child rearing, and social relationships. In the twentieth century, the South's striking degree of religiosity led to the region being dubbed America's "Bible Belt."

Likewise, sports and special forms of music promoted southern unity and identity. Having had a long tradition of physical display and aggressive competition, southerners eagerly embraced the rapid growth of organized sports in the post–Civil War era. Baseball came first. By the 1890s, every town of any consequence had one or more teams. The adoption of yet another northern game—football—by southern colleges and universities became an even more effective vehicle for the reassertion of state and regional pride. Teams adopted the colors of the Confederacy; they sought the imprimaturs of legendary figures from the region's past and symbolic regional victories through football victories over northern foes. Discontented people from both races helped to make the South what historian Edward L. Ayers has aptly described as "the crucible for the blues, jazz, and country music." Through a complex process of adaptation and invention, a set of young southern musicians, who began to come of age in the 1880s and 1890s, created a distinctive culture of regional music. In time, the influence of this culture would extend throughout the world.

Section Four

"African Americans and the Rights Revolution"

From Chapter 10 of *American Ways: A Brief History of American Culture*

Pages 238-242

THE RIGHTS REVOLUTION

Of its many complex and frequently opposing departures from the past, nothing was more central to the arrival of the new individualism than a revolution in rights. Prior to the sixties, rights had consisted of a finite body of entitlements enjoyed mainly by white men. But, beginning in the fifties with the civil rights movement and continuing into the sixties and long thereafter, the modernist urge for individual fulfillment encouraged one aggrieved group after another—African Americans, women, Native Americans, Hispanics, gays, welfare recipients, the handicapped, the elderly, and even consumers (among others)—to press forward claims for equality, relief from discrimination, and additional opportunities. Not only did these groups obtain greater recognition and a growing body of legal protections, but the rights revolution also brought with it far-reaching rearrangements in American race, ethnic, and family relationships.

A convergence of circumstances helped to set the stage for the rights revolution. One was a declining concern by the mid-1950s with domestic anticommunism. Few Americans objected when the U.S. Senate censured Senator Joseph McCarthy in 1954 or when in the late fifties the U.S. Supreme Court began to strike down the Cold War legal restrictions on "subversive" speech and associations. Even more corrosive to the postwar restraints on demands for an expansion of individual rights was economic abundance. As it had not done since the 1920s, the economy's performance opened up for millions previously unimaginable vistas of greater self-fulfillment; it made possible an exceptionally large, affluent youth culture; and it encouraged rising expectations among the less privileged. In short, general prosperity underwrote the innovation and daring that marked the new individualism while at the same time minimizing its risks.

AFRICAN AMERICANS AND THE RIGHTS REVOLUTION

No cause was more central to the rights revolution than that of African Americans. The black civil rights movement not only swept aside a long-established system of *legal* segregation and discrimination, but it affirmed in a spectacular fashion the modernist values of tolerance and pluralism. Sensitizing and heightening consciousness of repression, it also furnished a model for the organized movements of other discontented groups.

By the end of World War II, not much had changed since the turn of the twentieth century in the nation's system of race relations. As had been the case in 1900, law everywhere in the South still mandated the physical separation of blacks and whites in nearly all public situations. Segregation ranged from baseball parks and telephone booths to buses and classrooms. Neither could most African Americans vote in the South. And everywhere in the nation, housing segregation, either legal or de facto, was the rule. As late as 1960, of the fifty-two thousand people living in the model suburb of Levittown, Long Island, not one was known to be black. Job discrimination also existed everywhere. No matter where they lived in America, African Americans at mid-twentieth century could daily feel the awful sting and humiliation of being treated as inferior human beings.

In retrospect, the precipitants of a massive assault on the nation's traditional ways of race are clear. They include the "Double V" campaign—victory over the Axis Powers abroad and victory over racism at home—sponsored by black newspapers during World War II. They include the massive migration of African Americans from the southern countryside to the cities. The new urban dwellers helped to make possible the important symbolic breakthrough of the integration of major league baseball by Jackie Robinson in 1947, and they became a major component of the Democratic party coalition sympathetic to black rights. The precipitants of the civil rights revolt include the rise of new African states and the demand for ethnic and racial inclusiveness during and after World War II. They include a decided shift in educated white opinion. By the 1940s few white intellectuals any longer subscribed to theories of racial inferiority. In principle if not always in practice, modernist whites endorsed the ideal of success based on talents rather than skin color. A poll taken in 1956 revealed that 75 percent of white college graduates outside the South favored the racial integration of the schools.

Initiatives for the postwar assault on traditional racism came from several quarters. One was from the urban-centered National Association for the Advancement of Colored People. Responding to a suit brought by the NAACP, in 1954 a unanimous U.S. Supreme Court reversed its *Plessy* v. *Ferguson* decision of 1896. In *Brown* v. *Board of Education,* the court ruled that school segregation violated the equal protection of the law guaranteed to each citizen by the Fourteenth Amendment. Reflecting a characteristically modernist mindset, the court cited in support of its ruling a body of social science research. According to the findings of scholars, African-American children suffered irreparable psychological damage from the experience of school segregation. Hence, separate schools prevented African Americans from fully realizing their individual potentialities. Americans with modern values (including many in the urban South) applauded the *Brown* decision while traditionalists everywhere saw it as jeopardizing the American way of life.

Another major initiative for change came from African Americans living in the urban South. They found a leader in Martin Luther King, Jr., an eloquent young black minister. A product of both southern black Christianity and a northern modernist education, King brilliantly blended the old with the new. He repeatedly called upon an ages-old trope of black Christianity, the story of a divinely inspired Moses leading the children of Israel out of Egyptian bondage and into the promised land of Canaan. Echoing the abolitionists of the antebellum era, he called on higher law. Whenever man-made law, such as segregation statutes, contradicted higher law, he wrote in his *Letter from Birmingham Jail* (1963), then it should be resisted by nonviolent means. He drew upon the existentialist theology of Martin Buber. Segregation, King argued, diminished human individuality. By substituting an "I-it" relationship for an "I-thou" relationship between peoples, segregation allowed whites to perceive of and to treat blacks as things or objects rather than as human beings. By taking the movement into the streets, the new medium of television aided King's cause. On nightly television news shows, King's peaceful resistance and moderation stood in sharp contrast to the violence of local police, the inflammatory rhetoric of segregation's supporters, and the partiality of southern courts.

Comprised of blacks and whites, civil rights demonstrations reached a massive crescendo in the summer of 1963. During one week in June, police arrested more that fifteen thousand demonstrators in 186 cities. Demanding both an expansion of freedom and more black jobs, that summer a quarter of a million people (including a substantial white minority) marched on Washington. There, on the steps of the Lincoln Memorial, Martin Luther King, Jr., announced his "dream that one day ... the sons of former slaves and the sons of former slave-owners will be able to sit together at the table of brotherhood."

One vital ingredient was still missing from the movement. This was political leadership. Lyndon Johnson, a Texan who became president by virtue of Kennedy's assassination in 1963, filled that vacuum. The Civil Rights Act of 1964 and the Voting Rights Act of 1965, both unthinkable at the beginning of the decade, struck heavy blows at the legal bases of segregation. A far less noticed but an almost equally striking example of the startling advances of modern pluralism was the Immigration Act of 1965. The new act ended the national quota system that had long stigmatized Southern and Eastern Europeans as well as Asians. When combined, these acts represented gigantic steps in realizing more fully the egalitarian principle found in Thomas Jefferson's assertion in 1776 that "all men are created equal."

Lyndon Johnson not only presided over these momentous triumphs of egalitarian principle, but he contributed to the rights revolution in other ways. Building upon the ideas of freedom from want and freedom from fear that FDR had enunciated in his famed Four Freedoms speech in 1941, Johnson implicitly urged the impoverished and the elderly, among others, to see economic and medical security as a right or an entitlement. It was no longer enough, said Johnson in 1965, to think of equality of opportunity only in terms of eliminating discrimination that barred upward mobility. In "the next and more profound stage of the battle for civil rights ... we seek ... not just equality as a right and a theory, but equality as a fact and as a result." In

Martin Luther King, Jr., at the March on Washington in 1963. Such a massive demonstration on behalf of civil rights and jobs for African Americans would hardly have been conceivable a decade earlier. Other groups seeking liberation from traditional constraints drew upon the civil rights movement for inspiration and tactics.

an effort to move the country in this direction, the national government enacted the largest domestic agenda since the New Deal. It included a "war on poverty" program, medicare, medicaid, and increased federal expenditures on education.

In the meantime, the civil rights movement had polarized the nation. From the outset, traditionalist opponents had believed that racial differences were embedded in biology, the Bible, and in custom; hence, they thought that it was sheer folly for humans to think they could or should alter existing racial relationships. Throughout the South massive resistance greeted the *Brown* decision, and the peaceful marches, sit-ins, and mass arrests that King and his followers had used so successfully earlier in the South utterly failed to dismantle the North's black ghettos. A year before his death by an assassin's bullet in 1968, an incredulous King said he had never "seen as much hatred" as he encountered when he tried to integrate the white ethnic enclaves of Chicago. He confessed that open housing and equal employment opportunities for blacks remained "a distant dream."

Other blacks gave up on King's modernist goal of a racially integrated society. Drawing on the nationalist tradition of Marcus Garvey, Malcolm X, a leader of the Nation of Islam, rejected alliances with sympathetic whites or federal assistance; he insisted that blacks must rely on their own resources. The slogan of "Black Power" struck an especially responsive chord among young black activists. While never winning many victories nor carefully articulated, Black Power encouraged racial separatism. A similar separatist impulse would lead Native Americans, Chicanos, and third-generation ethnics to retreat from modern pluralism's inclusionist goal.

In the heady atmosphere of the mid-1960s few anticipated the degree to which racial separation would long afterward characterize American life. With the passage of the civil rights acts, administrative initiatives, affirmative action, and favorable court decisions, most modernists assumed that blacks would experience a rapid improvement in income, education, and integration into the larger society. But, while a significant minority of African Americans did achieve striking gains, many others remained far behind the national average in all indicators of equality with whites. At the end of the twentieth century, race seemed to remain the nation's most salient and persistent social and cultural division.

Section Five

"Social Movements in American Politics"

From Chapter 6 of *American Government: Political Change and Institutional Development*

Pages 155-160

From *American Government: Political Change and Institutional Development*, 2nd edition, by Cal Jillson, copyright 2002.

formal institutions is the best way to secure movement gains and build power for future battles.

Others point out that violent eruptions by social movements are usually short-lived. They flare up, maybe force changes and reforms, and die out. Unless movements leave institutions behind, there will be no one to monitor and protect the gains once the civil unrest dies away. For most movements, like the women's movement, the environmental movement, and the religious right, the need to have continuous institutional presence between movement peaks makes sense.

SOCIAL MOVEMENTS IN AMERICAN POLITICS

05 What common theme or "frame" did the social movements of the 1960s and '70s use to press their demands upon American society?

Social movements arise out of the effect that socioeconomic development has on prominent social divisions, including religion, race, ethnicity, gender, and lifestyle preference. Often compatible movements cooperate and coalesce as a wave of collective action passes through the society. The mid-nineteenth-century movements in favor of woman's suffrage, abolition, and temperance often shared members, leaders, and resources. Similarly, the mid-twentieth-century movements for nuclear disarmament, peace, and civil rights shared members, resources, and even protest strategies.

Students of social movements argue that both the surge in movement activity during particular periods and the similarities between movements that occur simultaneously are explained by the presence of a dominant **frame** or organizing theme. The frame of the revolutionary period was liberty, from England, from established churches, entrenched elites, and hierarchy in general. The frame of the mid-nineteenth century—free labor, entrepreneurship, and the right to contract—bound together the woman's movement, the labor movement, and the **abolition** movement. The civil rights revolution of the mid-twentieth century, in which most racial and ethnic groups, women, the disabled, the elderly, and many others joined, was built around the equal rights frame.[23]

Social movements designed to break through the barriers of race and gender have occurred throughout American history and marked progress has been made. We will analyze the social movements of the mid-twentieth century that demanded and to some extent achieved changes in the roles of race and gender within American society. Neither movement was entirely successful. Social movements rarely achieve all of their aims. We will ask how and why these social movements arose, gained momentum, achieved their early success, and then declined before their final goals were reached. We will also analyze the role of violence as used by and against social movements in America.

The Civil Rights Movement

The movement to end slavery in America had its origins in the debate over how threats to freedom and liberty justified revolution and political independence. Nonetheless, it took more than three-quarters of a century—and massive effort by growing numbers of people, black and white—before freedom for black slaves became a major issue in American national life in the 1860s. The Civil War brought an end to slavery and the adoption of amendments to the Constitution that promised equality with whites to the former slaves. The promise of equality was not kept.

By the turn of the twentieth century Jim Crow segregation had excluded most southern blacks from the electorate and from meaningful economic opportunity. In 1900, 90 percent of blacks lived in the South, and 87 percent were employed in agriculture or domestic service. Most of those in agriculture were working land owned by others and were frequently in debt. Three factors—the decline of cotton as the South's leading cash crop, the continuing rise of northern industry, and the slowing of immigration into the United States after 1910—led to massive changes in black America.

Five million blacks left the rural South mainly for the urban and industrial North between 1910 and 1960, three million after 1940. Nearly 90 percent settled either in California or in six industrial states of the middle Atlantic and upper Midwest—New York, New Jersey, Pennsylvania, Ohio, Illinois, and Michigan. Most found work in industrial, laboring, or service jobs. These jobs provided higher incomes than had their previous agricultural jobs, and the concentrated urban settings facilitated the growth of church, community, and fraternal organizations.[24]

Organization and Protest. The organizational base of the civil rights movement in the first half of the twentieth century was in the established institutions of the black community. Key among these were black churches, black schools and colleges, and the southern chapters of the National Association for the Advancement of Colored People (NAACP). These institutions provided tight social networks, access to established community leaders, and opportunities for bloc recruitment of congregations, student bodies, and local chapters into movement activities.

Movement activity often seemed to shift from one organization's base to the next. In the 1930s, '40s, and '50s the legal activities of the NAACP were the leading edge of the civil rights movement. Throughout this period an accelerating cycle of black protests and positive federal and northern state and local government responses produced a growing sense of black hope and possibility. As Piven and Cloward note, "each concession, however rhetorical, conferred legitimacy on the goals of the struggle and gave reason for hope that the goals could be reached, with the result that protest was stimulated all the more."[25]

Perhaps the most memorable mass protest campaign of this era was the 1955–1956 Montgomery bus boycott initiated by the refusal of Rosa Parks to give up her bus seat to a white man. For three hundred and eighty-one days the black citizens of Montgomery refused to ride the city buses and used their churches to organize alternative carpools and to coordinate their resistance to white pressure to end the boycott. The success of the Montgomery bus boycott did a great deal to demonstrate to both blacks and whites that resistance was possible and that sufficient resources and resolve existed in the black community to make resistance successful even against intense white opposition. Moreover, because the movement was built on a tightly

Thurgood Marshall (center) led the legal efforts of the NAACP. Here, the NAACP legal team arrives at the U.S. Supreme Court on December 11, 1952, to argue the famous school-desegregation case, Brown *v.* Board of Education.

Segregation required the separation of the races in most public settings. In this bus, whites are seated from the front and blacks are seated from the rear.

knit social network of churches, colleges, and civil rights groups, word of victories and of how they were won spread quickly, and successful tactics were copied elsewhere.

Nonviolence and Integration. Nearly a decade of successful mass action culminated in the summer of 1963 with the famous March on Washington and Martin Luther King Jr.'s "I Have a Dream" speech. A quarter of a million black and white supporters of desegregation and equal treatment for blacks gathered around the Tidal Basin at the foot of the Lincoln Memorial to demand decisive federal action on behalf of civil rights. The Kennedy administration responded with civil rights legislation that was dramatically strengthened by President Lyndon Johnson in the wake of the Kennedy assassination.

On the evening of November 27, 1963, President Johnson said to a joint session of Congress, "We have talked long enough in this country about equal rights. It is time now to write the next chapter—and to write it in the book of law." The 1964 Civil Rights Act and the 1965 Voting Rights Act represent the high tide of the integrationist phase of the civil rights movement. However, even as the marchers dispersed there were dynamics at work that led to the urban riots of the late 1960s, to white backlash, and to the demise of the movement.

The Rev. Martin Luther King Jr. addresses the March on Washington on August 28, 1963.

President Johnson and the Congress endorsed, through their words and their actions, the integrationist, equal rights agenda of the traditional civil rights organizations and their leaders. Full inclusion in the national mainstream, beginning with racial integration, was the fundamental goal of the civil rights movement of the mid-1960s. This phase of the movement dealt with fairly straightforward and easily identified problems, including segregated schools, buses, lunch counters, parks, and other public facilities, as well as blatant denial of the right to register and to vote. These discriminatory practices were impossible to disguise and relatively easy to solve through federal government action.

By 1966 a major gap opened within the civil rights movement between those who continued to pursue the mainstream integrationist agenda and others willing to move beyond nonviolence and integration to violence and separatism. Winning federal support for civil rights and the right to vote steered integrationists into traditional political and electoral activities and undermined the legitimacy of further protest and demonstration. Others questioned the presumed gains, asking how important it is to be permitted to eat in a restaurant, or enroll in a college, or live in a neighborhood, if you cannot afford the meal, the tuition, or the house.

Racial Violence and Black Nationalism. Poor blacks in the northern cities were largely bypassed by the integrationist phase of the civil rights movement. In the urban ghettos of the northern cities talk of equal rights and integration seemed hollow. The real problems were inadequate housing, poor schools and high illiteracy, high unemployment and low pay, crime, and white flight to the suburbs. These circumstances produced a series of violent urban uprisings throughout the late 1960s.

Advocates of black power, such as Stokely Carmichael, rejected integration as the main goal of black protest and advocated adoption of "any means necessary" to achieve justice for black people. Carmichael asserted that, "integration is irrelevant. Political and economic power is what black people have to have."[26] More broadly, the black power wing of the movement questioned the basic desirability of integration with the white majority, questioned nonviolence as the only strategy available to the movement, and questioned the presence of white liberals in the leadership of the movement.

This substantive shift in the thinking and rhetoric of at least a substantial wing of the civil rights movement posed a significant threat to established political and economic interests in the country. White and black liberals were concerned by the rhetorical and physical violence, and white conservatives were concerned by the overt challenge to their status and values. The backlash was quick and stern.

Support among whites for civil rights went into a steep decline from which it has never recovered. Whites responded as if the good-faith efforts represented in the civil rights and voting rights legislation of the mid-1960s had been betrayed. Many citizens and politicians who were reluctant to attack equal rights were quite comfortable calling for "law and order" and for the stern suppression of crime and violence. In 1968 Republican Richard Nixon adopted "law and order" rhetoric to ride white middle-class disaffection with the Democrats and their civil rights agenda into the White House.

Section Six

"Civil Rights and the Civil War Amendments"

From Chapter 13 of *American Government: Political Change and Institutional Development*

Pages 370-379

From *American Government: Political Change and Institutional Development*, 2nd edition, by Cal Jillson, copyright 2002.

CIVIL RIGHTS AND THE CIVIL WAR AMENDMENTS

Civil liberties protect areas of social interaction where individuals are to be left free to do as they please. Civil rights protect areas of social interaction where the state ensures that each individual has the same opportunity. Before the Civil War, civil liberties and civil rights seemed to be roughly the same thing, and for white men they were quite similar. The distinction became clearer after minorities and women began to claim the same liberties and rights available to white men.

The distinction came powerfully to the fore in the famous case of *Dred Scott* v. *Sandford* (1857), in the Civil War amendments to the Constitution, and in the Civil Rights Act of 1875. Chief Justice Roger B. Taney, writing for the Court in the *Dred Scott* case, declared that white slave owners were at liberty to do as they wished with black slaves because blacks had "no rights which the white man was bound to respect." Dred Scott, a black slave from Virginia, was taken to Missouri and then by a new owner to the free state of Illinois and later into the free territory of Wisconsin. Taney declared not only that Scott was not free as a result of being carried into free territory, but also that no black, slave or free, was a citizen either of a state or of the United States.

The Thirteenth, Fourteenth, and Fifteenth Amendments to the Constitution, the Civil War amendments, were designed to assure former slaves that they did, in fact, have "rights that the white man was bound to respect." Active government intervention to assure that these rights were acknowledged and respected was obviously necessary. The Civil Rights Act of 1875 was part of the national government's attempt to define civil rights for post–Civil War America.

The Civil War Amendments

President Abraham Lincoln described the Civil War as "essentially a people's contest. [A] struggle for maintaining in the world that form and substance of government whose leading object is to elevate the condition of man—to lift artificial weights from all shoulders; to clear paths of laudable pursuit for all; to afford all an unfettered start, and a fair chance in the race of life."[11] A little more than two years later he set the end of slavery in motion with the Emancipation Proclamation.

Not until after the war did the Republican party in Congress begin to define the rights that the former slaves would enjoy and how those rights would be guaranteed and protected. The Civil War amendments and the Civil Rights Act of 1875 laid out a promise of full equality. However, within little more than a decade all of these promises had been broken. By the end of the century "separate but equal" was constitutional doctrine, and by 1910 an American apartheid, Jim Crow segregation, was in place across the land.

The Thirteenth Amendment: Freedom. The Thirteenth Amendment completed the work of emancipation. It reads: "Neither slavery nor involuntary servitude, except as a punishment for crime whereof the party shall have been duly convicted, shall exist within the United States, or any place subject to their jurisdiction." The Thirteenth Amendment went into effect on December 18, 1865.

The Fourteenth Amendment: Equality. The Fourteenth Amendment sought to define, without ever mentioning them directly, the position of the former slaves within the American society. The key section of the Fourteenth Amendment reads: "All persons born or naturalized in the United States, and subject to the jurisdiction thereof, are citizens of the United States and the State wherein they reside. No State shall make or enforce any law which shall abridge the privileges or immunities of citizens of the United States; nor shall any State deprive any person of life, liberty, or property, without due process of law; nor deny to any person within its jurisdiction the equal protection of the laws." This broad and generous language went into effect on July 28, 1868.

The Fifteenth Amendment: Voting. The Fifteenth Amendment sought to ensure that black citizens would be able to defend their rights and liberties at the ballot box. The Fifteenth Amendment, which went into effect on March 30, 1870, read: "The right of citizens of the United States to vote shall not be denied or abridged by the United States or any State on account of race, color, or previous condition of servitude." The vote, it was hoped, would be a powerful weapon that could be wielded in defense of rights and privileges awarded in the previous two amendments. For a time it seemed that this would be so, but that time proved to be very brief.

Early Supreme Court Interpretations. Almost before the ink was dry on the Civil War amendments the Supreme Court interpreted them in the narrowest possible terms. Soon thereafter the Civil Rights Act of 1875 met the same fate. Precisely how the words of the Civil War amendments and the Civil Rights Act of 1875 were made tools of continued oppression and exclusion of blacks, rather than powerful tools for black equality, can be shown by looking at several key Supreme Court decisions.

The first decision did not even involve blacks. Nonetheless, its implications for the place of the newly freed blacks in the American society were immense. The *Slaughterhouse Cases* (1873) were brought by a group of white New Orleans butchers who claimed that the creation of a slaughterhouse monopoly by the Louisiana state legislature denied them the equal protection of the laws that the Fourteenth Amendment promised them as citizens of the United States.

What then were the rights of U.S. citizens? Justice Samuel F. Miller, writing for the majority of a Court divided 5–4, announced a strict dual-federalist view that saw national and state citizenships as essentially separate. Under Justice Miller's reading, national citizenship protected a citizen while traveling abroad, engaging in interstate or foreign commerce, or engaging in activities not within the jurisdiction of a single state. All other rights belonging to Americans as citizens belonged to them as citizens of particular states. The *Slaughterhouse Cases* announced that state governments would be allowed to define the domestic rights of their citizens, including their black citizens, as narrowly as they wished and that the federal government would not interfere.

The first major test of the Civil Rights Act of 1875, which made most racial discrimination illegal, whether practiced by public institutions like governments or by private individuals, came in a set of cases known as the *Civil Rights Cases* of 1883. In an 8–1 decision, Justice John Marshall Harlan I dissenting, the Supreme Court declared the Civil Rights Act of 1875 to be unconstitutional. Justice Joseph P. Bradley explained that in the view of the Court the Fourteenth Amendment prohibited discriminatory "state action" against blacks, it did not prohibit and could not reach the private discrimination of one individual against another. With this judgment the federal government withdrew from the fight against private discrimination against blacks.

***Legal Segregation:* Plessy *v.* Ferguson.** In 1890 the state of Louisiana passed a law requiring railroads to "provide equal but separate accommodations for the white and colored races" and requiring that "no person be permitted to occupy seats in coaches other than the ones assigned to his race." Homer Plessy, a citizen of Louisiana and one-eighth black, set out to test the laws by boarding a train and occupying a seat in a car designated for white passengers. Following Plessy's arrest, his lawyer argued that the Louisiana statute violated the Thirteenth and Fourteenth Amendments, and most particularly the "equal protection" clause of the Fourteenth Amendment. The Court upheld the Louisiana statute and, by implication, most other segregation statutes, noting that "the action was not discriminatory since the whites were separated just as much from blacks as the blacks were separated from the whites."

Justice Harlan rose in vehement dissent, pointing first to the obvious hypocrisy of the claim that segregation by race was no "badge of inferiority" for blacks subjected to it. Justice Harlan then went on to state the case for black equality that he believed to be inherent in the Thirteenth and Fourteenth Amendments. He explained that "there is in this country no superior, dominant, ruling class of citizens. . . . Our Constitution is colorblind, and neither knows nor tolerates classes among citizens. In respect of civil rights all citizens are equal before the law. The humblest is the peer of the most powerful. The law regards man as man, and takes no account of his . . . color when his civil rights . . . are involved." It would be more than half a century before these powerful words would be accepted by a majority of the nation's highest court.

The Civil Rights Movement

The early twentieth century was a bleak time for civil rights in America. Not until the 1930s did forces begin to build both domestically and internationally that put the country on the road to desegregation by midcentury. However, looking back on the successes and failures of the modern civil rights movement, many Americans, both blacks and whites, are struck both by how much has changed on the surface and by how little has changed beneath the surface.[12] Many are sobered by the slow progress of equality and by the backsliding toward segregation that has occurred over the past two decades.

***Desegregation: The Coming of* Brown *v.* Board of Education.** The road that led from *Plessy* v. *Ferguson* to *Brown* v. *Board of Education* was long and painful. Assignment of children to schools on the basis of race was upheld as late as 1927 when the Supreme Court let stand a decision by the state of Mississippi that Chinese children could not attend the white schools and had to attend the black schools within the state. However, the legal tide began to turn in the 1930s.

Missouri, like several other border states and all of the states of the Deep South, ran a dual, or segregated, school system from kindergarten through college. However, as with most other segregated education systems, Missouri's did not provide a full range of advanced and professional degree programs at its black institutions. Therefore, upon graduation from Missouri's all-black Lincoln University, Lloyd Gaines sought admission to the University of Missouri's Law School. Gaines was denied admission, though he was informed that the state of Missouri would pay the cost of his attending law school in an "adjacent state." Gaines sued, claiming that his right to "equal protection of the laws" under the Fourteenth Amendment had been violated. The Supreme Court agreed and informed the state of Missouri that it had to provide a separate law school or admit blacks to the

University of Missouri Law School. The state responded by setting up a law school at Lincoln University.

Two landmark cases from 1950 raised the question of how equal separate facilities had to be. In *Sweatt* v. *Painter* the Court held that a law school set up to avoid admitting blacks to the University of Texas Law School was unacceptable because it was inferior in facilities, books, faculty, and in general quality of legal education and opportunities. *McLaurin* v. *Oklahoma* struck down an attempt to admit blacks to a white program on a "segregated basis." McLaurin was admitted to the University of Oklahoma's School of Education to pursue graduate study because no black universities in the state offered similar programs. However, he was restricted to a seat in an anteroom adjacent to the classroom and to an assigned space in the library and the cafeteria. The Court supported McLaurin's contention that this treatment denied him "equal protection of the laws."[13]

The precedents established in *Gaines, Sweatt,* and *McLaurin* made the point that if facilities are to be separate, they must truly be equal. But could separate in fact be equal? In the landmark case of *Brown* v. *Board of Education of Topeka, Kansas* (1954) the U.S. Supreme Court was asked to take up precisely this question: Can separate be equal, or is separate inherently unequal and therefore discriminatory within the meaning of the "equal protection" clause of the Fourteenth Amendment? A great deal, including the entire post-*Plessy* segregation of the American society, was at stake in *Brown* v. *Board.* Arguing for the black complainants was Thurgood Marshall, chief counsel of the National Association for the Advancement of Colored People (NAACP).

Brown v. *Board of Education* was before the Court when conservative Chief Justice Fred M. Vinson died and was replaced by the liberal Republican former governor of California, Earl Warren. Chief Justice Warren, like Thurgood Marshall, thought that segregation had to be dismantled and that *Brown* was the right case to begin that process. Writing on behalf of a unanimous Court, Warren reached back to resurrect Justice Harlan's dissent in *Plessy.* Warren wrote that, "Segregation of white and colored children in public schools has a detrimental effect upon the colored children." Therefore, Warren concluded, "in the field of public education the doctrine of separate but equal has no place. Separate educational facilities are inherently unequal. . . . The plaintiffs . . . have been deprived of the equal protection of the laws guaranteed by the Fourteenth Amendment."

Thurgood Marshall

When the decision in *Brown* was released to the public on May 17, 1954, seventeen states and the District of Columbia mandated segregation in their elementary and secondary schools. Although the District of Columbia and most of the border states complied with the instruction to desegregate their schools, the states of the Deep South dug in for a decade-long contest called "massive resistance." As late as 1960 not a single black student attended a public school or university with whites in Alabama, Georgia, Louisiana, Mississippi, or South Carolina. Moreover, when John Kennedy took the oath of office as president of the United States early in 1961, fewer than 4 percent of voting-age blacks in Mississippi were registered to vote. The numbers were only slightly higher in the other southern states.

The Civil Rights Acts: 1964, 1965, and 1968. The Kennedy administration came under increasing pressure on the civil rights front during the "long, hot, summer" of 1963. That summer culminated in the famous March on Washington in which two hundred thousand people participated. The highlight of the march was Martin Luther King, Jr.'s, "I Have a Dream" speech delivered from the steps of the Lincoln Memorial. The Kennedy administration responded to the demands of Dr. King and his followers by preparing legislation to supplement the Eisenhower administration's Civil Rights Act of 1957. That bill, the first major piece of civil rights legislation since Reconstruction, had established the U.S. Civil Rights Commission and enhanced the Civil Rights Division of the Department of Justice.

http://www.usdoj.gov/crt
CIVIL RIGHTS DIVISION OF THE DEPARTMENT OF JUSTICE

In the wake of President Kennedy's assassination in November 1963, President Lyndon Johnson dramatically strengthened Kennedy's civil rights bill. The new bill came to be known as the Civil Rights Act of 1964. Its critical Title VI held that "No person in the United States shall, on the ground of race, color, or national origin, be excluded from participation in, be denied the benefit of, or be subjected to discrimination under any program or activity receiving Federal financial assistance."

Title VII of the act prohibited discrimination on the basis of race, color, sex, religion, or national origin by employers or labor unions in businesses with one hundred or more employees; prohibited segregation or denial of service based on race, color, religion, or national origin in any public accommodation, including motels, restaurants, movie theaters, or sports facilities; and permitted the U.S. attorney general to represent citizens attempting to desegregate state-owned, -operated, or -managed facilities, including public schools.

An even more far-reaching civil rights act was passed in 1965, as was the Elementary and Secondary Education Act (ESEA) of 1965. The ESEA provided federal education funds to school districts with large numbers of low-income students. These funds could be denied if schools were found to be discriminating. Finally, in April of 1968, only days after the assassination of Martin Luther King, Jr., Congress passed a law that forbade discrimination based on race, color, religion, or national origin in the sale or rental of housing.

The provision of federal money to support state and local programs, especially in education, seemed to break the back of segregation. Gerald Rosenberg has noted that "financially strapped school districts found the lure of federal dollars irresistible. . . . And after federal money was received, the thought of losing it the next year, reducing budgets, slashing programs, firing staffs, was excruciating."[14] The most striking result of the movement of the Congress and the executive branch into the fray over desegregation was that the percentage of black school children attending school with whites in the South rose from 1.2 percent in 1964 to 91.3 percent in 1972.

The Voting Rights Act of 1965. The foundation of **Jim Crow** had been the near-total exclusion of blacks from southern state and local electorates and their limited participation in northern elections. A complicated array of rules and practices, including literacy tests, poll taxes, white primaries, and grandfather clauses, kept blacks, other minorities, and the poor more generally, from registering and voting in elections.

Specifically, the Voting Rights Act of 1965 prohibited the further use of literacy tests and other practices deemed to have a discriminatory impact. It sent federal marshals into southern states to assure that local election officials permitted all citizens to register to vote and to participate in elections. By 1970 ten million new black voters were on the rolls, and by 1984 black registration had passed white registration at 73 percent to 72 percent of those eligible. Large numbers of registered black voters simply could not be ignored by politicians expecting to remain in office.

Affirmative Action

05 Does affirmative action to assist minorities or women automatically and inevitably mean reverse discrimination against white men?

The civil rights agenda of the 1950s and 1960s demanded equality of opportunity and nondiscrimination. These ideas were embedded as promises and guarantees in the civil rights and voting rights acts of the mid-1960s. **Affirmative action** envisions making up for the effects of past discrimination suffered by specified racial and sexual groups by giving their members preference today in admission to training and educational programs and in decisions concerning hiring, promotion, and firing on the job.

Redressing Direct Discrimination. Is government responsible for ensuring nondiscrimination now and in the future, or is it also responsible for making up for the effects of past discrimination? The Civil War Congress considered seizing plantations owned by Confederate loyalists, break them up into lots of "40 acres and a mule," and distributing them to the newly freed slaves. This proposal was based on the understanding that the newly freed slaves would be unlikely to succeed unless the government acted "affirmatively," giving them an economic stake upon which to build. Former slave owners had benefited directly from the labor of their former slaves. Even so, white Americans were unwilling to see the property of other white Americans, even southern rebels, taken for redistribution to former slaves.

Similarly, the Civil Rights Act of 1964 was carefully crafted to apply only to **direct discrimination** against identifiable individuals by other identifiable individuals and to prohibit racial preferences or "affirmative action." Proponents of the Civil Rights Act of 1964 were very clear in assuring skeptical colleagues that the act offered protection not to broad classes of people but only to specific individuals who could show that they had suffered direct discrimination as a result of racial bias. Moreover, numerous provisions of the Civil Rights Act of 1964 seemed specifically to prohibit racial quotas or hiring goals that might result in reverse discrimination against whites.

Claims of Reverse Discrimination. The first and most famous **reverse discrimination** case was decided in 1978 and involved a man named Allan Bakke. Bakke was twice rejected for admission to the University of California at Davis Medical School even though on both occasions his academic credentials were superior to those of all

PRO *and* CON

SEARCHING FOR A COLOR-BLIND SOCIETY: NONDISCRIMINATION, AFFIRMATIVE ACTION, AND REVERSE DISCRIMINATION

Proponents of affirmative action argue that nondiscrimination and equality of opportunity, although certainly important, are radically insufficient to assure the full and meaningful participation of blacks and other minorities in the American society and economy. They argue that the current unequal status of blacks in America, to take the prime example, is a stark reflection of two centuries of slavery in which the products of black labor were stolen by white slave owners and another century in which Jim Crow segregation was used to deny blacks access to opportunity and wealth. Yet, even if one approves of affirmative action to redress the destructive legacies of slavery and segregation, one still has to think about the kind of affirmative processes to use and how long they should remain in place.

Opponents of affirmative action argue for a nondiscriminatory or color-blind society in which persons are judged on their merit rather than on their race or gender. Practicing nondiscrimination and judging people on their merit, regardless of their race or gender, sounds right. After all, slavery and segregation were abhorrent because they penalized people, black people, merely because of the color of their skin. But how right and fair can it be for the people of one race, whites, to hold the people of another race, blacks, in subjection for three centuries, taking or severely limiting their access to opportunity and wealth, finally and only grudgingly to agree to stop the oppression (say, somewhere between *Brown* v. *Board of Education* in 1954 and the Civil Rights Act of 1964), and then within a decade, a mere ten years, to begin to grumble about "preferences" being given to blacks?

Opponents of affirmative action object to policies that they regard as "reverse discrimination." These delicate issues were treated, generally in favor of affirmative action, in several critical Supreme Court decisions of the late 1970s and early 1980s. More recently, however, the Supreme Court has restricted the use of racial preferences in admission to educational institutions, in the awarding of financial aid, and in contract set-asides in the private sector.

How should we think about the issue of treating fairly today and in the future those members of our society who, we know, were treated unfairly in the past?

of the minority students admitted under the school's affirmative action program. The medical school, like many other graduate and professional schools, set aside a number of seats, in this case sixteen out of about one hundred, for minorities and took the best minority candidates available. The remaining seats were awarded to the top candidates based on their academic credentials. Bakke sued the University of California at Davis Medical School and, in a case known as *Regents of the University of California* v. *Bakke,* won—sort of.

Justice Lewis Powell, writing for a badly divided Supreme Court, held that the university had violated Bakke's Fourteenth Amendment right to equal protection of the laws and that he should be admitted to the medical school. Specifically, the Court held in a narrow 5–4 decision that institutions could not set aside a specific number of seats for which only minorities were eligible. This stark denial of opportunity for whites to compete for these seats was unconstitutional. The Court further held, however, that race could be used as a positive factor in admission decisions if it were not the sole factor.

One year after *Bakke* came *United Steelworkers of America* v. *Weber.* Kaiser Aluminum and the United Steelworkers had agreed that at least half of the thirteen slots in an on-the-job training program at Kaiser's Gramercy, Louisiana, plant would go to blacks. Brian Weber was denied a place in this training program on the basis of his race—he was white—so he sued the company and the union under Title VII of the Civil Rights Act of 1964. Title VII expressly prohibited discrimination in employment, forbidding any employer from granting "preferential treatment to any individual or to any group because of the race . . . of such individual or group."

Justice William Brennan upheld the affirmative action agreement reached by Kaiser and the United Steelworkers as a "voluntary" and "temporary" attempt by parties in the private economy to benefit black workers. Brennan argued that although the "letter" of the Civil Rights Act of 1964 required nondiscrimination, its "spirit" permitted voluntary agreements designed to improve the lot of blacks in the American economy. Justice William Rehnquist, writing in dissent, accused the Court of rejecting race-blind in favor of race-conscious standards for government policy-making and private behavior.

Justice Rehnquist was even more dismayed by the Court's 1980 decision in the case of *Fullilove* v. *Klutznick.* In 1977 Congress passed a $4 billion public works bill that included language requiring that 10 percent of the funds be set aside for "minority business enterprises." Chief Justice Burger, though he had dissented in *Weber,* wrote the majority opinion for the Court in which the set-aside provision was upheld as a legitimate "temporary" measure undertaken by Congress to redress the wrongs of the past. Rehnquist argued that the "Fourteenth Amendment was adopted to insure that every person must be treated equally by each State regardless of the color of his skin. . . . Today the Court derails this achievement and places its imprimatur on the creation once again by government of privilege based on birth."

The Rights of Protected Classes. Two cases from 1986 and a third from 1987 extended the idea of job preferences for members of **protected classes** and made them applicable to women. One of the 1986 cases dealt with public sector workers,

Cleveland city firefighters, whereas the other dealt with private sector workers, New York sheet-metal workers. In these cases the Court made clear that businesses and agencies may favor protected-class workers in hiring and promoting whether or not workers could show that they were victims of individual discrimination. Moreover, the Court declared that federal judges could set goals and timetables for employers to redress the effects of past discrimination and that state agencies can go beyond court-ordered measures in their attempts to act affirmatively.

In the 1987 case of *Johnson* v. *Transportation Agency, Santa Clara County,* the Court reaffirmed that public and private employers could take race and sex into account in making their personnel decisions. *Johnson* was the first time that the Court approved an affirmative action plan giving job preferences to women. "The Court unambiguously held that *without any proof of past discrimination* against women and minorities by a particular employer, the latter may use racial and sexual preferences in hiring and promotions to bring the workforce into line with the local population or labor market."[15] By the late 1980s nondiscrimination had transformed into affirmative action and then into preferences for protected classes.

The early 1990s, on the other hand, saw affirmative action come under increasing pressure. In 1995 the Supreme Court invalidated a University of Maryland program that set aside a certain number of scholarships exclusively for minorities and a federal program that gave minority highway construction contractors an advantage in competing for work.[16]

The 1997 case of *Piscataway Board of Education* v. *Taxman* raised the issue of how far a public employer can go to achieve and maintain racial diversity in the workforce. The Piscataway school board was faced with the need to reduce its workforce by one math teacher. Two teachers, one black, one white, equally qualified and with equal seniority, were on the bubble. The school board members argued that racial diversity of the faculty was a legitimate goal, so they laid off the white teacher, Sharon Taxman. Taxman sued under Title VII of the 1964 Civil Rights Act, which forbids discrimination in employment. After two lower courts ruled that the school board did, in fact, violate Ms. Taxman's civil rights, several civil rights organizations financed a private settlement of the suit so that the Supreme Court could not use it to decisively limit affirmative action. Stay tuned—this issue is still very much alive.

Section Seven

"Prejudice"

From Chapter 7 of *Our Social World*

Pages 233-271

Prejudice

The four men were about to become antagonists in a violent drama on the frozen winter streets of Boston. Cuneo was driving a battered Comet, and his buddy Boyle sat by his side. They were keyed up after working as bouncers at a local bar, very drunk, and white. On a nearby street, Booker was driving a maroon Buick with a weak battery. Wilson, Booker's neighbor, was sitting next to him: the two of them were headed for home after working a shift at the nearby medical center. They were tired, sober, and black.

The Comet and the Buick were sitting side by side at a red light at Park Square when Boyle rolled down his window and began shouting insults at Booker; his language was obscene and laced with racial epithets. When Booker answered back with his own opinions of Boyle and his heritage, Cuneo waded into the melee by spitting at Booker. The incident would have ended when the light changed and Cuneo sped off if Booker's Buick hadn't stalled. Cuneo made a U-turn on the dark street so he could drive back and renew the conflict. By then, Booker was connecting jumper cables to his stalled car. Wilson stood by his side. Boyle immediately rushed the pair, and Booker responded by pulling out a baseball bat from under the Buick's front seat. Boyle then snatched up the jumper cables and began to swing them in Booker's face. Meanwhile, Cuneo, still in his car, tried to run over Wilson, who ran down the street and around the corner.

The white men were winning the battle. One witness explained, "It was all their show" (Sedgwick, 1982, p. 158). But when the jumper cables slipped from Boyle's February-frozen fingers, Booker closed in. Pulling a knife from his coat, he buried the blade in Boyle's liver:

> Boyle stumbled back a few steps, then straightened and hobbled back to the Comet. He told Cuneo his side hurt, then passed out. Thinking Boyle had been clubbed with the bat, Cuneo reached under his friend's sweater to feel his ribs. When he pulled out his hand, it was covered with blood. (Sedgwick, 1982, p. 158)

Cuneo rushed Boyle to a nearby hospital, but Boyle didn't live through the night.

prejudice
Liking or disliking people because they belong to an ethnic, racial, or other social category one likes or dislikes; prejudice usually refers to a negative bias rather than a positive one.

Boyle was killed by his own **prejudice**: his intense rejection of another person simply because that person belonged to a group he disliked. Countless groups comprise modern society—young, old, blacks, whites, Anglos, Latinos, men, women, Arabs, Israelis, Catholics, Protestants, gays, straights, Coke drinkers, Pepsi drinkers, and on and on. In many cases, people develop strong attitudes toward the members of these groups. In theory, prejudicial attitudes can be positive biases, but the term usually carries a negative connotation. As we see in the first section of this chapter, prejudice implies an unfavorable rejection of others that is both unfair and irrational. It prompts us to *prejudge* people solely on the basis of their membership in a group or category. Boyle did not see two individuals with unique personality traits, interests, and goals when he looked out his car window and saw Booker and Wilson. Instead, he saw two black men, and he hated them.

Recognizing the prejudiced nature of Boyle's attitudes and actions is not enough, however. We must also explore the roots of his prejudice and attempt to discover why, across many societies and many eras, the people in one group have hated the people in other groups. Was Boyle's antagonism part of his basic personality—a closed-minded person who resisted new ideas and social change? Did his intolerance spring from a general antipathy for anyone who didn't belong to the same social group or category that he did? Or did he reject black people because white society had taught him to think of African Americans as targets of abuse and hatred? Prejudice has many causes, but once we enumerate them, we can turn to a more hopeful topic—cures for prejudice.

The Nature of Prejudice

The 19th-century English author Charles Lamb admitted, "I am, in plainer words, a bundle of prejudices—made up of likings and dislikings—the veriest thrall of sympathies, apathies, and antipathies." Mark Twain, however, claimed that he was completely unprejudiced: "I have no race prejudices, and I think I have no color prejudices nor creed prejudices. Indeed, I know it. I can stand any society."

Are you prejudiced? Before deciding, consider the meaning of the term to a social psychologist. Experts do not agree on how to define the term most clearly, but prejudices are, above all else, attitudes. So, as the tri-component model of attitudes discussed in Chapter 6 suggests, prejudices actuate our feelings, our thoughts, and our actions (see Figure 7-1). The *affective component* of prejudice is characterized by emotions that range from mild nervousness to outright hatred. Such statements as "I hate whites," "Allowing gays in the army makes me angry," "Blacks frighten me," and "I can't stand pushy women" all illustrate the emotions in our prejudices. Indeed, our strongest negative emotions are often reserved for groups rather than individuals. As Gordon W. Allport (1954) noted in his classic treatise, *The Nature of Prejudice,* "anger is customarily felt toward individuals only, whereas hatred may be felt toward whole classes of people" (pp. 340–341).

Prejudice also includes a *cognitive component*: assumptions and beliefs about the members of other groups. These cognitions can be as inaccurate as our emotions are ardent, but we feel that these beliefs are supported by facts and objective observations. An American citizen who is prejudiced against Russians, for example, may assume Russians deserve this rejection because they are untrustworthy, aggressive, and unintelligent. A racist Anglo may believe that Latinos are lazy. Such overgeneralizations about the members of other social groups are **stereotypes**. As discussed in Chapter 3, stereotypes are cognitive schemas, so they can systematically influence our perceptions and memories.

stereotypes
Socially shared generalizations about people who are members of a particular group or social category.

discrimination
Differential treatment of a person based on his or her membership in an ethnic, racial, or other social category.

Discrimination constitutes the *behavioral component* of prejudice. A sexist man, for example, may quit his job when he is transferred to a department managed by a woman. A prejudiced black may discriminate against whites by treating them unfairly. The behavioral component of an attitude, however,

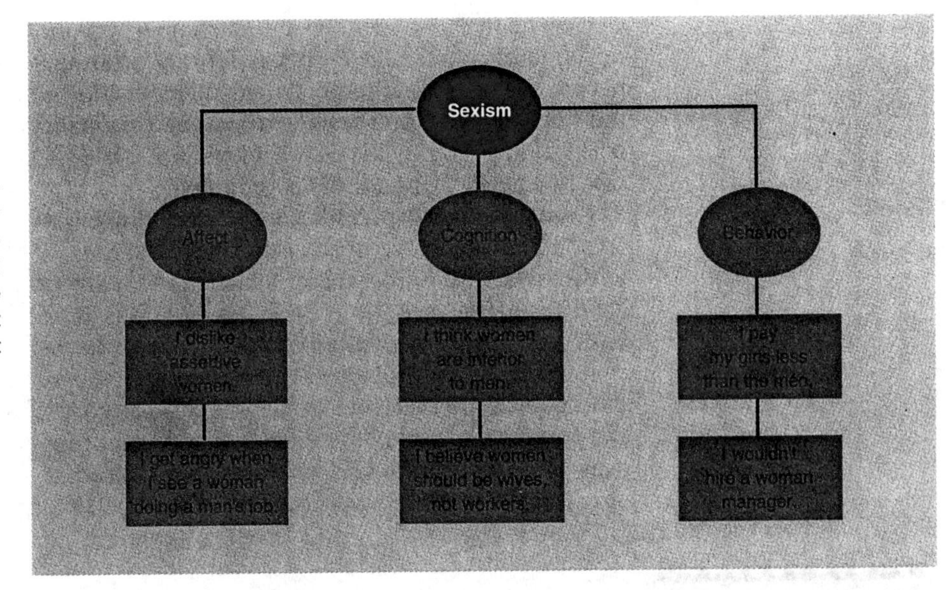

▲ **FIGURE 7-1**
What is prejudice? The tricomponent theory of attitudes argues that prejudice, like any other attitude, includes emotions, thoughts, and actions. This model suggests that prejudices such as sexism occur when individuals experience negative feelings toward women, endorse unfavorable beliefs and assumptions about women, and act in ways that discriminate against women.

also includes predispositions to respond in certain ways. A white person who is prejudiced against African Americans could plan to live in segregated housing areas and decide to vote for only white candidates in all elections. (Varying views on the definition of prejudice are offered by Ashmore & DelBoca, 1981; Brewer & Kramer, 1985; Duckitt, 1992; Simpson & Yinger, 1985.)

Prejudice can be directed at virtually any one of the innumerable groups that make up our heterogeneous society. Even today, Catholics, Jews, Muslims, and other religious groups are persecuted for their beliefs. Those who adopt alternative lifestyles, such as gays and lesbians, are often the victims of prejudice-motivated violence: so-called *hate crimes* or *bias crimes*. People who are physically challenged are viewed in stereotypical ways that are both demeaning and unfair. Latinos, Asian Americans, Native Americans, and other ethnic and racial groups experience systematic persecution because they are different from others. All of these forms of prejudice demand close study, but we cannot survey the vast literature on all these forms of prejudice in one chapter. We therefore concentrate on only two of these many forms of prejudice, in detail: **racism**, which is prejudice based on race, and **sexism**, or prejudice based on biological sex. This emphasis on racism and sexism does not mean that other forms of prejudice are less important or less worthy of study.

racism
Prejudice against people based on their membership in a racial category.

sexism
Prejudice against people based on their biological sex (either male or female).

Racial Prejudice

Racial tensions and prejudices have long been a part of American society. In colonial times African men, women, and children were enslaved by European whites, who denied them any rights of justice or equality. The passage of three amendments to the U.S. Constitution restored some of their civil rights, but African Americans were still systematically oppressed by unfair labor laws, voting restrictions, and exclusionary practices. Throughout the early 1900s, black people were considered to be inferior in many ways, and **apartheid** laws prohibited equal status or intimate contact between the two groups. Then, in 1954, the U.S. Supreme Court struck down many of these unfair laws in *Brown* v. *Board of Education of Topeka, Kansas*. The Court mandated the desegregation of public schools, but progress was negligible until the social movements of the early 1960s forced the passage of new civil rights legislation. Now, some

apartheid
A political system based on racial segregation and discrimination.

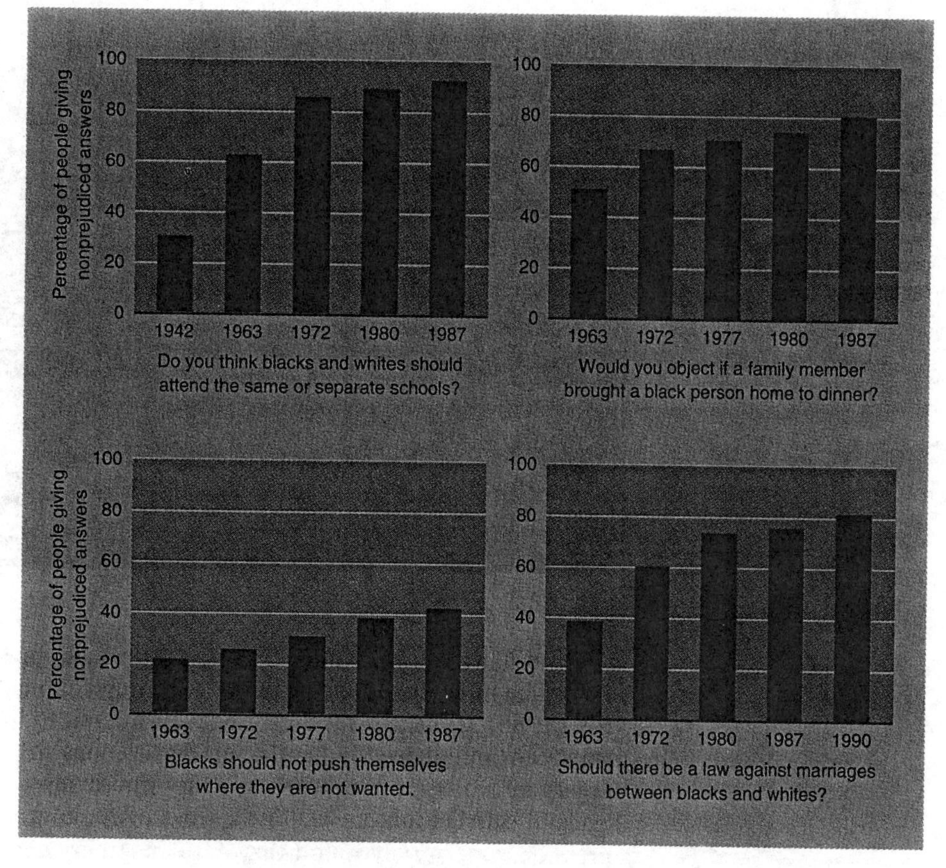

▲ **FIGURE 7-2**
Have white Americans' attitudes toward blacks changed in the last 50 years? Public opinion polls suggest that whites were highly prejudiced in the early 1940s: most felt that blacks and whites should attend separate schools, that contact between the two groups should be minimized, and that intermarriage should be illegal. Over the years, however, whites' attitudes have become increasingly egalitarian. (Data from Davis & Smith, 1990)

40 years after the Court's ruling, treating a person unfairly because of his or her race or color is neither legal nor condoned.

Have white people's attitudes kept pace with these changes in civil rights? Polls taken between 1942 and 1990 are heartening. In 1942, most white Americans favored segregated schools and separate seating areas on streetcars and buses (see Figure 7-2). In 1944, most white people felt that a white should be given the chance to take a job before it is offered to a black. In 1958, only 37% of white voters said they would vote for a black man for president if their party nominated him. In 1963, 50.4% of white Americans surveyed claimed they would object if a member of their family brought home a black friend to dinner; 63.6% felt that interracial marriage should be against the law; and 78.2% felt that blacks shouldn't "push themselves where they're not wanted." These numbers, however, changed dramatically during the 1970s and 1980s. Now, well over 90% of white people accept black people in schools, their homes, neighborhoods, and public office. White racists, once the majority in America, are now the minority (Schuman, Steeh, & Bobo, 1985; Wood, 1990).

Other evidence, however, is less encouraging. As Figure 7-2 indicates, some whites still express openly negative attitudes toward African Americans. As recently as 1992, 36% of the white Americans polled by Gallup (1993, p. 92) agreed that "many whites dislike blacks," and 35% of the African Americans agreed that "many blacks dislike whites." Second, hostile encounters between blacks and whites—like the savage attack perpetrated by Boyle—may be increasing rather than decreasing. Police officials recorded 15 separate bias incidents during a 9-day period in January of 1992 in New York City alone. The vicious beating of Rodney King by police officers reaffirmed to many the lack

▲ White Americans' attitudes toward African Americans have become more positive over the years, but conflict between the two groups still remains. Nearly 20% of all white Americans are prejudiced against African Americans, and many African Americans report feelings of economic, social, and political oppression.

of racial harmony in America, and set the stage for the Los Angeles riots of 1992. The number of blacks killed by whites doubled between 1978 and 1988 (FBI, 1988). College campuses, once considered to be safe harbors in a sea of American prejudice, frequently serve as venues for racial conflicts. Last, the targets of whites' prejudice—African Americans—continue to report lower levels of satisfaction, as well as feelings of economic, social, and political oppression. One survey found that African Americans continue to feel discriminated against when seeking housing, jobs, and a good wage (Sigelman & Welch, 1991). In another survey, 42% of the black respondents opined that whites want to keep blacks in their place; 36% stated that white people do not care what happens to black people. Most blacks in the United States identify more closely with African blacks than with whites in America (Institute for Social Research, 1983).

These figures suggest that anti-black racism in America has changed during the last 30 years. The white racist who openly denounces blacks and favors segregation may be a rarity, but many experts believe that new forms of prejudice have supplanted traditional prejudice (Kleinpenning & Hagendoorn, 1993). Contemporary forms of white racism, including covert racism, aversive racism, symbolic racism, and regressive racism, are examined next.

Covert racism. The white salesclerk doesn't like waiting on African Americans but knows that it's just part of the job. The white grandmother believes schools should be segregated, but talks about these ideas only with her daughter. The honors student thinks the blacks in his classes are stupid, but he does not say so. Such **covert racism** occurs because some whites continue to be prejudiced against blacks, but they keep their sentiments hidden from public scrutiny to avoid the appearance of racism (Batson et al., 1986).

covert racism
Prejudice against members of other racial categories, which is not expressed openly.

Researchers must use more sensitive methods of measurement than opinion polling to detect covert racism. One such method, the *bogus-pipeline procedure,* involves convincing people that their truthfulness is being monitored by a highly accurate lie-detector machine. Subjects first fill out a questionnaire pertaining to such innocuous issues as movies, sports, and music.

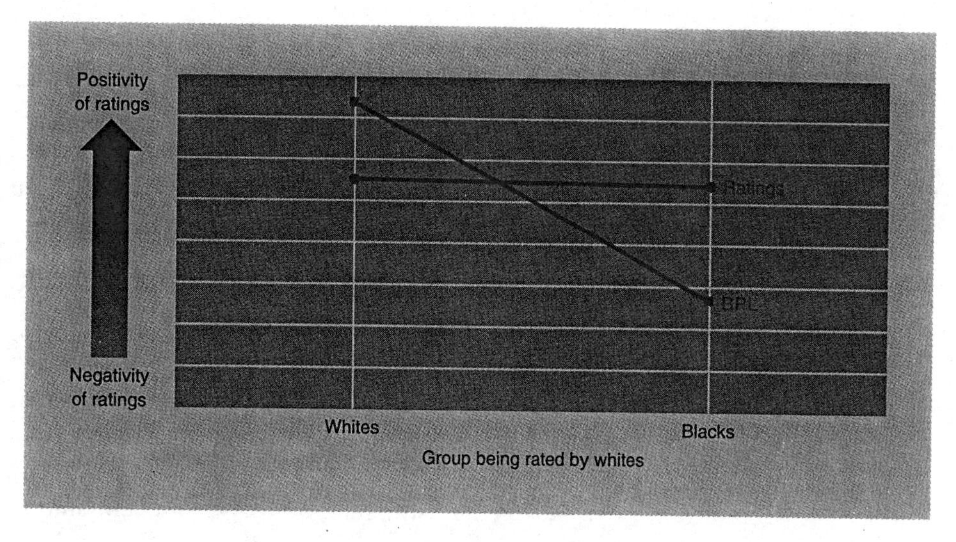

▲ **FIGURE 7-3**
Do white people claim to be less prejudiced than they actually are? When whites rated blacks' and whites' intelligence, stupidity, sensitivity, dirtiness, and other qualities, they showed no signs of prejudice. The overall index of their ratings for blacks was as positive as their overall ratings of whites (as the line labeled "Ratings" indicates). But when they thought dishonesty would be detected by a lie-detector machine (the BPL), their ratings of whites were much more positive than their ratings of blacks. (From Sigall & Page, 1971)

Next, the experimenter connects them to a maze of sophisticated equipment. The researcher claims the machine measures attitudes as accurately as a lie-detector test. He or she then demonstrates the machine's precision by asking subjects a few questions about movies, sports, and music. After each question, the machine buzzes momentarily, then spits out its reading of their opinion. Amazing space-age technology? Not really. The machine's dials and buzzers are controlled by a confederate in the next room who has a copy of the subjects' responses to the original questionnaire (Jones & Sigall, 1971; Roese & Jamieson, 1993).

When connected to the bogus pipeline, people give more prejudiced answers than people who fill out questionnaires or answer a pollster's questions. The white college students in one study were asked whether African Americans are intelligent, honest, lazy, talkative, musical, ambitious, and so on. They rated white Americans as well. A second set of subjects completed the same ratings while connected to the pipeline. The method of measurement made a critical difference, as Figure 7-3 indicates. Students who thought that any dishonesty would be detected by the bogus pipeline rated blacks more negatively than whites, whereas students who used the paper-and-pencil methods rated the two groups identically. The researchers concluded, "Current stereotypes: A little fading, a little faking" (Sigall & Page, 1971, p. 247).

Covert racism also surfaces when people believe they are interacting with like-minded individuals. When whites in one study watched two people debate the issue "the value of nuclear energy," they rated a black who lost the debate as favorably as a white who lost the debate. A different pattern emerged, however, when a confederate in the audience made a racial slur just before the ratings were taken. When the accomplice used a racist word to describe the black man, the subjects rated the losing black debater more negatively than the losing white debater (Greenberg & Pyszczynski, 1985). Similarly, when students gave their opinions about a series of racial incidents on campus after hearing another person condemn those involved, they agreed that the perpetrators should be punished. If, however, the other person condoned the mistreatment of black people, then the students were much less likely to condemn the perpetrators. Indeed, in some cases, these students expressed approval of white students who harassed black students (Blanchard, Tilly, & Vaughn, 1991).

Aversive racism. How will you respond when you pick up the ringing phone in your home or dorm room and the voice on the line says:

> "Hello . . . Ralph's Garage? This is George Williams. . . . Listen, I'm stuck out here on the parkway . . . and I'm wondering if you'd be able to come out here and take a look at my car." (Gaertner & Bickman, 1971, pp. 219–220)

When you tell George that he has the wrong number, he exclaims:

> This isn't Ralph's Garage! Listen, I'm terribly sorry to have disturbed you, but listen . . . I'm stuck out here on the highway . . . and that was the last dime I had! I have bills in my pocket, but no more change to make another phone call. . . . Now I'm really stuck out here. What am I going to do now?
>
> Listen, do you think you could do me the favor of calling the garage and letting them know where I am? I'll give you the number. . . . They know me over there. (Gaertner & Bickman, 1971, pp. 219–220)

Would you make the call for George and help him out, or would you just forget about it?

Samuel Gaertner, John Dovidio, and their colleagues believe that your response may be tinged by your racial prejudices. Using this *wrong-number technique,* they called 1109 residents of Brooklyn, New York, between 6:30 and 9:30 P.M. and made the request. After hanging up, the researchers waited for the subjects to call the number for Ralph's. They identified their subjects' sex and race using location of residence, last name, and voice characteristics. Seven blacks, who purposely spoke in a southern black dialect, and 7 whites made the telephone calls. White listeners, as Figure 7-4 shows, discriminated more than blacks. They helped whites 12% more frequently than blacks, whereas blacks helped whites 7% more frequently than blacks (Gaertner & Bickman, 1971).

Gaertner and Dovidio believe that many whites are fair-minded: they sincerely strive to treat others justly. Many, however, continue to experience aversive emotions when they interact with African Americans. These negative feelings, which include nervousness, stress, tension, and concern, are vestiges of nearly forgotten racial fears and anxieties, and in many cases they aren't even consciously recognized. Such individuals may swear that they are unprejudiced—that they are color-blind when it comes to race—yet they respond

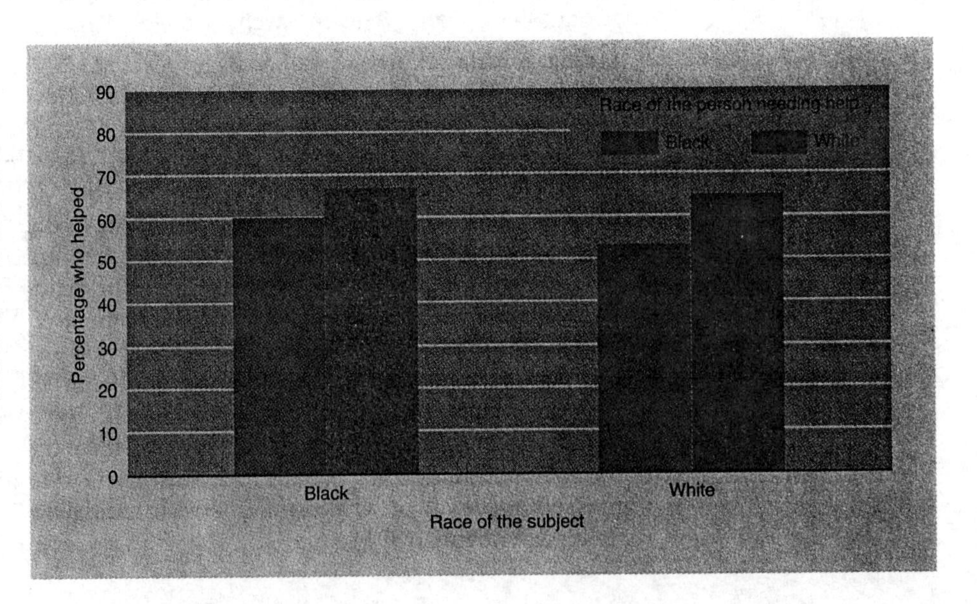

▲ FIGURE 7-4
If a man calls you on the phone and asks for help, would you be more likely to agree if he was a member of your racial group? When a white asked for help, race made no difference. He was helped by equal numbers of African Americans and whites. But when an African American asked for help, white racism surfaced. Whites were more likely to help a white person than a black person. (From Gaertner & Bickman, 1971)

▲ Blatant racism has declined in recent years, to the point that overtly racist acts (such as KKK cross-burnings) are relatively rare. This old-fashioned, overt racism has been replaced by more subtle forms of racism, such as aversive racism. Whites who experience aversive racism don't express their prejudice overtly, but they nonetheless experience negative emotions when they encounter African Americans in public places. As Kenneth B. Clark concludes, modern prejudice is "more complicated and more subtle."

aversive racism
Prejudice experienced by individuals who accept egalitarian values but nonetheless experience negative emotions in the presence of members of other racial groups.

negatively to black people. Gaertner and Dovidio call this bias **aversive racism**: a negative emotional reaction to members of another group experienced by people who endorse nonprejudicial values. Like the subjects in the wrong-number study, aversive racists may hang up the phone without listening when the caller is black. They help a white who has fallen down, but they overlook a black person who needs help (Gaertner & Dovidio, 1986). They brusquely shake off the request of a black petitioner, but they stop and listen to the white petitioner's request for a signature (Crosby, Bromley, & Saxe, 1980). They are animated and personable when they are interacting with a black person, but privately they feel upset and uncomfortable (Ickes, 1984). When asked whether they are prejudiced, these individuals claim that they are not; yet they choose to sit by a white rather than a black on a crowded bus or pass by a black panhandler to give a coin to a white one (Dovidio & Gaertner, 1986, 1991).

Symbolic racism. Dick argues that blacks have only themselves to blame for their poverty—if they just worked harder, they could overcome their problems. Darlene and Roberta think that African Americans, as a group, don't value a good education, so they often end up in dead-end jobs. John insists that anyone in America can succeed if they apply themselves (from interviews in Wellman, 1977). These individuals all show signs of **symbolic racism**, "a blend of anti-black affect and the kind of traditional American moral values embodied in the Protestant Ethic" (Kinder & Sears, 1981, p. 416). Symbolic racists tell themselves that they don't condemn a person based on his or her color or creed. They do, however, dislike people who reject traditional American values of individualism, self-reliance, discipline, and hard work. And blacks, they feel, fit this category (McConahay & Hough, 1976; Sears, 1988; Sears & Kinder, 1985).

symbolic racism
Prejudice displayed by individuals who claim they reject other racial groups, not because of their color or background, but because these other groups don't accept traditional social values.

The concept of symbolic racism explains why many white Americans enthusiastically endorse principles of racial equality but refuse to support the programs needed to implement these principles. They claim to bear no grudge against black people, but they object to government welfare programs ("Most people on welfare are just lazy"), hiring quotas based on race ("The government shouldn't interfere in a company's hiring practices"), and busing to

▲ **FIGURE 7-5**
Why are some whites so inconsistent in their dealings with blacks? Studies of symbolic racism suggest that some whites hold two sets of conflicting values—egalitarian and work ethic—and think blacks don't work hard enough. When symbolic racists consider egalitarian values, they rate blacks more highly and reject anti-black sentiments. But when they reflect on work-ethic values, their anti-black ratings increase, and pro-black scores fall slightly. (Data from Katz & Hass, 1988)

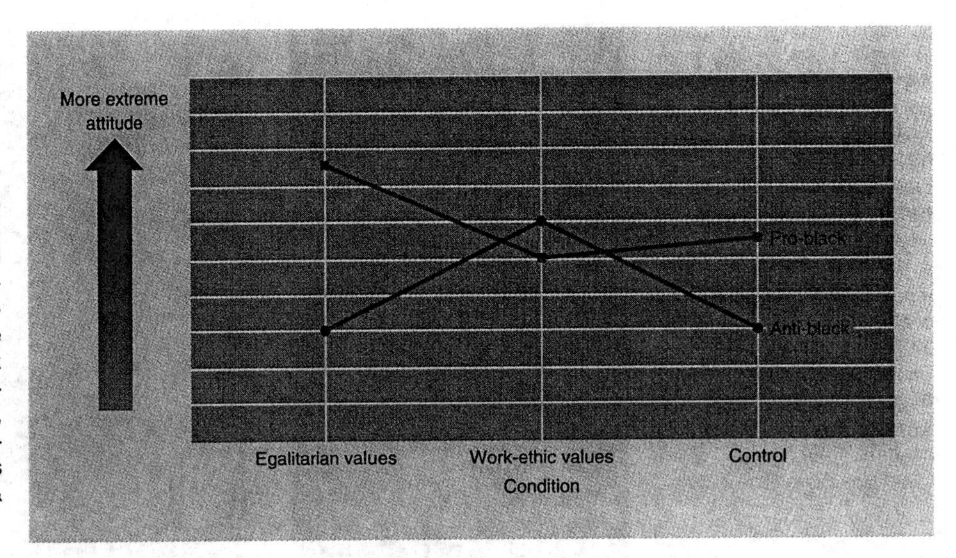

achieve integrated schools ("Kids should be able to go to neighborhood schools"). This principles-implementation gap stems, in part, from a general dislike of government regulations. However, it also reflects the belief that governmental assistance to blacks is unfair and undeserved (Institute for Social Research, 1985; Kinder & Sears, 1981).

Some researchers believe that symbolic racists unconsciously use their political values as justification for rejecting blacks. When people who don't want to be prejudiced find themselves reacting negatively to blacks, they explain away their responses by attributing them to their traditional values rather than to racial prejudices (McConahay, 1986). Other researchers, however, believe that many whites are continually struggling to balance their belief that everyone should be treated fairly and their belief that black people don't do enough to help themselves. These competing sets of values leave whites feeling profoundly ambivalent about African Americans, for they simultaneously feel that blacks are victims of decades of mistreatment *and* are undeserving of any assistance (Hass et al., 1991, 1992; Katz, 1981; Katz, Wackenhut, & Hass, 1986).

This ambivalence often translates into inconsistent patterns of discrimination and fairness when whites interact with blacks. When whites' egalitarian values (that is, principles of fairness) direct their reactions, they treat blacks fairly and without prejudice. When, however, their work-ethic values (such as individualism, self-reliance, discipline, and hard work) are dominant, then they respond negatively to blacks (see Figure 7-5). When whites first reflected on their egalitarian values before completing a measure of anti-black sentiment and pro-black sentiment, their pro-black scores climbed, and their anti-black scores fell. When they first reflected on their work-ethic values, however, the reverse occurred. Anti-black scores increased, and pro-black scores fell slightly (Katz & Hass, 1988).

Regressive racism. Why, to this day, does racism "bind the mind in such a way that democratic relationships in adult life are impossible" (Allport, 1954, p. 99)? Why, in 1989, did working-class whites in Brooklyn shoot a 16-year-old black youth who was visiting the neighborhood to buy a used car? Why did white police officers brutally beat Rodney King in 1991? Why did Boyle attack Booker?

▲ **FIGURE 7-6**
Will otherwise fair-minded whites react violently when angered by a black? When the whites in this study were insulted by a confederate of the researcher, they administered stronger and longer electric shocks when the insulter was black rather than white. Unangered whites treated blacks more favorably than whites. (From Rogers & Prentice-Dunn, 1981)

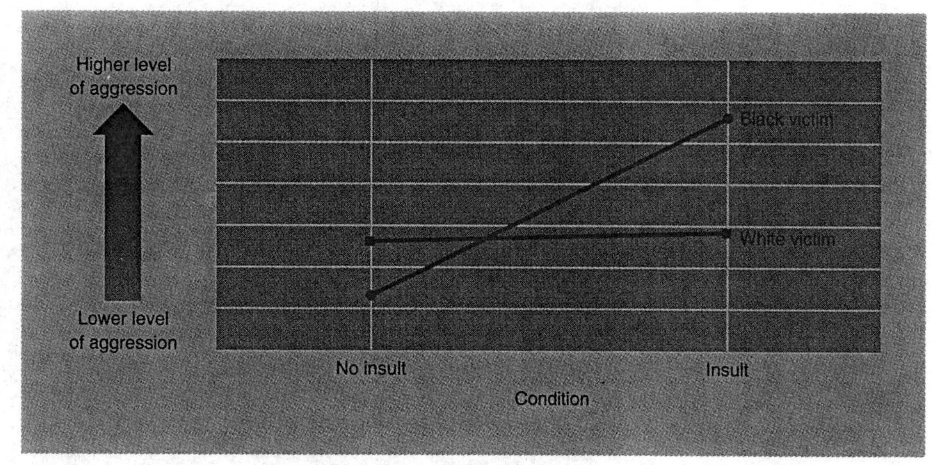

Ronald Rogers and Steven Prentice-Dunn (1981) theorize that most whites in America do not want to treat others unfairly, nor do they want to foster the impression that they are racists. Therefore, in most everyday situations, whites' personal prohibitions against acting in racist ways and the possibility that others will perceive them to be racist keep them from discriminating against blacks. When, however, these restraints are stripped away by feelings of anger, fear, or other arousing circumstances, whites act more impulsively. In extreme cases, they may even regress to an outmoded pattern of racial aggression that Rogers and Prentice-Dunn label **regressive racism**.

regressive racism
Open condemnation of or discrimination against members of another group that occurs when personal prohibitions against acting in racist ways are inhibited by emotions.

Rogers and Prentice-Dunn succeeded in documenting the link between anger and regressive racism in their laboratory. They told their white college student subjects that, as part of a study of behavior modification, the students would be asked to give painful electric shocks to another student. This other student, who was actually a confederate, had been sitting in the waiting area with the subjects before the study began. In some cases, a black student played the role, but in others, a white student took his place. Then, as the confederate was apparently being wired up to receive shocks, a second variable was manipulated. Sometimes the confederate deliberately insulted the subjects: He mentioned that the equipment looked complicated, and he wondered whether people who looked as dumb as the other subjects could use it properly. Sometimes he said nothing negative about the others. The confederate actually received no shocks, but the number and duration of the shocks meted out by the subjects was carefully recorded.

Rogers and Prentice-Dunn found that unangered whites responded very differently from angered whites (see Figure 7-6). Unangered white subjects treated whites more shabbily than blacks; they displayed a pattern of reverse discrimination (Baron, 1979; Donnerstein & Donnerstein, 1973; Griffin & Rogers, 1977). Angered whites, however, displayed regressive racism. They administered stronger and longer electric shocks to the black victim than to the white victim. Once their anger inhibited their personal prohibitions against acting in racist ways, they acted impulsively rather than rationally.

Contemporary white racism. Whites' attitudes toward blacks have changed a great deal since the early 1960s. Yet remnants of prejudice remain (see Table 7-1). Overt, blatant prejudice has decreased, but covert prejudice remains. Despite their best attempts to respond to others fairly, some whites experience aversive emotions when they interact with blacks. Still others fall

▲ **TABLE 7-1**
Summing up: Contemporary forms of racism

	Definition
Overt Racism	Open condemnation of the members of another group
Covert Racism	Public tolerance of the members of another group paired with rejection of this group privately, when detection is unlikely, or when prejudice is condoned by others
Aversive Racism	Acceptance of egalitarian values paired with unexamined negative emotional responses to members of the other group
Symbolic Racism	Acceptance of egalitarian and traditional work-ethic values combined with the belief that members of the other group do not act in accordance with traditional work-ethic values
Regressive Racism	Open condemnation of or discrimination against members of another group that occurs when personal prohibitions against acting in racist ways are inhibited by emotions

prey to symbolic racism because they assume that blacks' values differ from theirs. And some lose the fight against bigotry when their anger obscures their good judgment, and they display regressive forms of prejudice. As Kenneth B. Clark, a leading social psychologist in the field of racism, concludes, modern prejudice is "more complicated and more subtle" (quoted in Winston, 1983, p. D-3). Whites' attitudes are changing, but prejudice remains.

Prejudice Against Women

When Boyle died, the police arrested Booker *and* Wilson. Wilson explained that he was down the street fighting with Cuneo when Boyle was stabbed, but the police knew better. An attendant at a parking deck, who happened to be white, told a different story. He was nearly a block away, but he claimed that Wilson yelled, "Dig him" just before the stabbing. A second witness offered a different story, but the police did not believe her. Laura Mitchell explained that she watched the entire incident from just across the street. She claimed that the whites were the aggressors and that it was Cuneo who yelled, "Get him, get him." But the police dismissed her evidence entirely. She was, after all, contradicting the testimony of a man.

Attitudes about men and women have changed in many ways since the early 1900s. Women can now enter into contracts and own property without the consent of their fathers or their husbands. Women can also vote in elections, serve on juries, and run for public office. Indeed, as Figure 7-7 indicates, most Americans now claim that (a) they would vote for a woman for president if she were nominated by their party, and (b) they approve of a married woman who works even though her husband is capable of supporting her. Yet, just as the police officers assumed that Laura Mitchell was confused by the violence she witnessed, people continue to embrace stereotypes about women and men. These stereotypes, as we will see next, influence both perceptions of men and women *and* the treatment of men and women.

Stereotypes about men and women. The ancient book *I Ching* describes the fundamental forces of nature as yin and yang. Yin is woman: dark, the negative, emotionality, the passive, the feminine. Yang, in contrast, is man: light, the positive, rationality, the active, the masculine. Aristotle described women as more humane, more envious, more disagreeable, more moody, more "false of speech," and less self-respecting than men. In 1933, Sigmund Freud

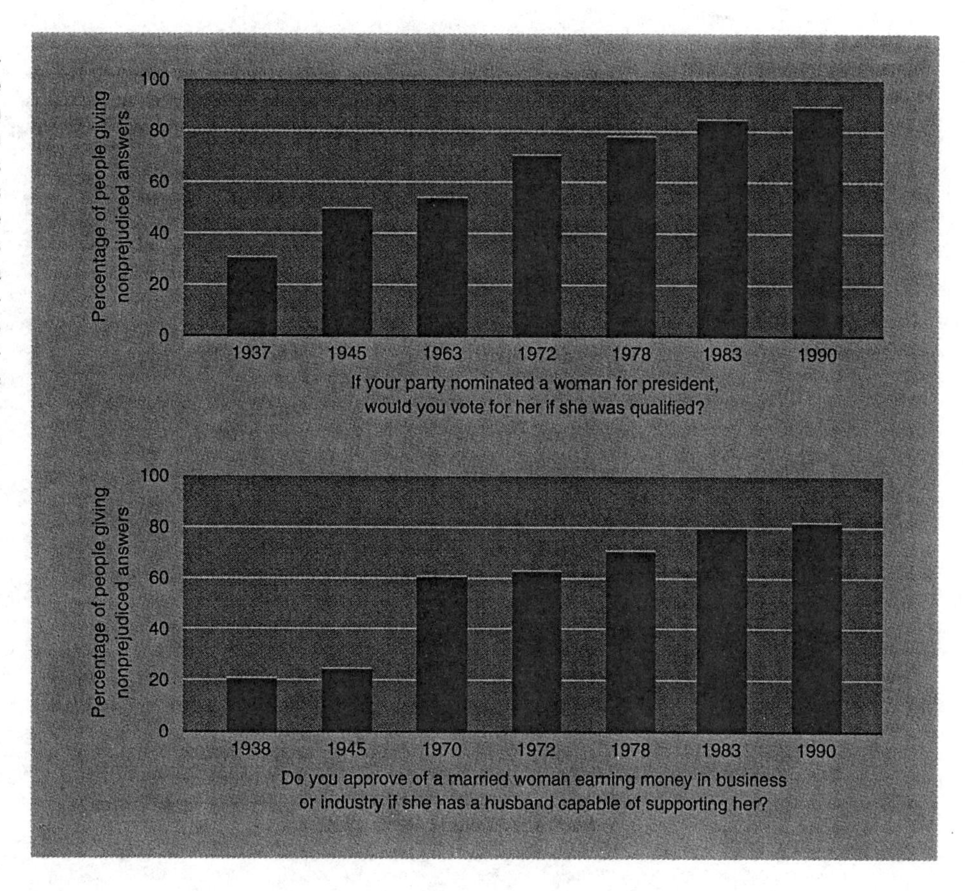

▲ FIGURE 7-7
Have Americans' attitudes toward women changed in the last 50 years? Public opinion polls suggest that opposition to women's taking active roles in politics and business has waned over the years. In the late 1930s, most Americans were opposed to the idea of a woman candidate for president or a woman business leader. By the 1990s, these attitudes gave way to become more and more egalitarian. (Data from Davis & Smith, 1990)

wrote: "It must be admitted that women have but little sense of justice, and this is no doubt concerned with the preponderance of envy in their mental life" (p. 183).

For centuries now, people have assumed that men differ from women in predictable ways. If we have never met a person before, but we know the person's sex, we can offer up a number of guesses about his or her other characteristics. Will Brian be indecisive or competitive? Will he be physically strong or weak? Will he enjoy shopping or watching sports? Do you think Tonya is independent or nervous? Is she athletic or frail? Is she skilled in business or an excellent cook? Even though we realize that sex differences are fading, we nonetheless use people's sex as a heuristic index of their personality traits, their physical attributes, and the roles they occupy in society (Deaux & Lewis, 1984).

Table 7-2 presents the 20 traits that were most frequently mentioned by people in their descriptions of men and women in 25 different countries (Williams & Best, 1990). Although gender stereotypes varied among the different cultures, two basic themes emerged with impressive consistency. When asked to describe women, people in virtually all cultures spoke of their *expressive* qualities, including nurturance, emotionality, and warmth. They expected a "she" to be sentimental, affectionate, sympathetic, soft-hearted, talkative, gentle, and feminine. When describing men, they stressed their *instrumental* qualities, including productivity, energy, and strength. Most expected a "he" to be boastful, ambitious, independent, strong, forceful, dominant, and masculine (Martin, 1987; Spence, Deaux, & Helmreich, 1985).

▲ **TABLE 7-2**
Terms most frequently used to describe men and women

When people in 25 countries were asked to describe sex-related qualities of men and women, the majority mentioned these qualities. Those listed at the top of the columns were mentioned more frequently than those further down the list, although all the adjectives were frequently mentioned.

Adjectives Used to Describe Women	*Adjectives Used to Describe Men*	*Neutral Adjectives*
feminine	handsome	adaptable
sentimental	enterprising	resentful
affectionate	tough	suspicious
sympathetic	opportunistic	withdrawn
soft-hearted	rational	peculiar
talkative	logical	dissatisfied
flirtatious	egotistical	bossy
attractive	assertive	hasty
gentle	courageous	bitter
appreciative	confident	intelligent
dreamy	daring	vindictive
fussy	boastful	alert
sensitive	ambitious	interests wide
excitable	independent	interests narrow
frivolous	strong	defensive
sexy	forceful	good-natured
warm	dominant	dependable
submissive	adventurous	clever
cheerful	aggressive	forgetful
fickle	masculine	planful

Source: Williams & Best, 1990.

Stereotypes aren't limited only to presumptions about personality traits. People also expect men and women to act differently and take on different kinds of social roles (Deaux & Lewis, 1984). Stereotyped thinking causes people to assume that men are more likely to be task- and activity-oriented: Men change the car's tire when it goes flat, they play competitive sports, they take charge and lead, and they are the financial providers for their families. Women, in contrast, are often thought to be interpersonally oriented: They cook the meals and clean the home, they take care of the children, and they resolve conflicts between family members (Deaux, 1984; Deaux & Major, 1987).

Do these stereotypes mirror real differences between men and women, or are they unfair myths? First, many stereotypes about women and men are simply false: the differences they describe don't exist. Systematic studies of sex differences in such areas as intelligence, leadership, and emotionality have failed to find differences between men and women (Eagly, 1987).

Second, even though gender stereotypes may contain a kernel of truth, these differences are not so profound that they can be used as a basis for making judgments about any specific man or woman. The sexes are different in some ways. Women are better at reading nonverbal messages (Hall, 1984), they are more sensitive to feedback from others (Roberts, 1991), and they tend to be happier than men (Wood, Rhodes, & Whelan, 1989). Men are more autocratic leaders than women (Eagly & Johnson, 1990), more aggressive (Hyde, 1986), and physically stronger (Thomas & French, 1985). These differences are a matter of degree rather than kind, however. Many men are sensitive to nonverbal messages, and many women are not. Similarly, many women are autocratic

▲ You have just met this woman at a party. Can you form an impression of her? Do you think she is warm and sensitive, or cold and blunt? Do you think she makes decisions quickly, or does she procrastinate before committing herself? If given a choice, would she like to go to a movie or to a baseball game? Is she a homemaker or does she work at a bank? Your answers to these questions may have been influenced by your stereotypes about women.

leaders, and many men prefer to adopt a more democratic style. Women and men aren't "opposite sexes" by any stretch of the imagination.

Last, even when the differences suggested by stereotypes can be documented, a final interpretational wrinkle remains. The stereotypes themselves may be causing the sex differences. Almost from birth, we are treated differently depending on our sex. Parents of newborns think that their baby girl is weak and fine-featured, but their baby boy is big and strong. Parents who see a baby crying assume that the child is angry when they think the baby's a boy, but they think the child is fearful when they think the baby's a girl (Condry & Condry, 1976). Mothers and fathers treat their sons and daughters differently, rough-housing more with the boys and encouraging their independence, while showing more affection and protection with girls (Lytton & Romney, 1991; Siegal, 1987).

Moreover, as Alice Eagly (1987) suggests, even as adults we can't escape the restraints of social conventions regarding the sexes. The woman who marries and has a child, for example, may not be very nurturant or caring. Once in the role of mother, however, she may become more nurturant as she meets the role's requirements. Similarly, a man may not be aggressive or competitive by nature, but if he enters a profession or occupation, his role may require him to act in these ways. Thus, stereotypes don't necessarily arise because people notice differences between men and women. Rather, differences between men and women arise because social roles and stereotypes create these differences.

Contemporary forms of sexism. The police officers' stereotypes about women and men didn't influence only their perceptions of Laura Mitchell. They also influenced the way they responded to her. They discriminated against her by dismissing her statements but wholeheartedly accepted the claims of the man who witnessed the fight. Sex stereotypes are not harmless misconceptions. They reinforce the continuing discrimination against women in contemporary society.

Just as the police officers devalued Mitchell's evidence, society in general tends to place a lower value on the qualities, actions, accomplishments, and roles that are associated with women rather than men.

Qualities ascribed to men are judged to be more socially desirable than those attributed to women. Stereotypical masculine qualities, such as independence, objectivity, rationality, and ambition, are more valued in many societies than are stereotypical feminine qualities, such as emotionality, warmth, and sentimentality (Rosenkrantz et al., 1968).

Actions performed by men are evaluated more positively than the identical actions performed by women. When, for instance, people are asked to evaluate men and women leaders, they give higher scores to the men, even when the men and women being reviewed performed identical behaviors (Brown & Geis, 1984; Butler & Geis, 1990; Geis, Boston, & Hoffman, 1985).

Accomplishments of women are evaluated more critically than men's accomplishments. For instance, in one study people who read an article that was supposedly written by Joan T. McKay rated it more harshly than people reading the same article attributed to *John* T. McKay (Goldberg, 1968). Meta-analyses of subsequent studies indicate that such blatant bias is relatively rare (Swim et al., 1989). More frequently, women's accomplishments are diminished only indirectly. When, for example, people hear that a woman has performed a task well, they often assume that her success was more a matter of luck rather than ability. Men's successes, however, are attributed to their abilities (Deaux & Emswiller, 1974).

Roles more frequently occupied by women tend to be viewed as less important than roles occupied by men. In most societies, the division of labor is based on sex: men usually generate income by working outside the home, whereas women carry out domestic tasks such as child-rearing and food preparation within the home. Note, however, that work outside the home is viewed as more difficult and more worthy of financial reward than work inside the home (Nielsen, 1990).

Sexism leads to economic disadvantages for women. Even though the number of women working outside the home has risen steadily over the years, men hold a near monopoly on the most financially lucrative professions and occupations (Roos, 1985). Women tend to be nurses rather than physicians, schoolteachers rather than administrators, legal secretaries rather than lawyers, and dental hygienists rather than dentists. In every case, occupations dominated by women are lower in prestige and salary than those occupied mostly by men. Moreover, even when women manage to enter a male-dominated field, their advancement in their profession is often slower than men's. A glass ceiling seems to block women's rise into top management positions. Women make up about 5% of the middle management and only 1% of the top management. A survey of corporate heads located 15 female chief executive officers (CEOs) and 2,500 male CEOs (Nielsen, 1990). In the well-known case of *Hopkins* v. *Price Waterhouse,* Ann Hopkins outperformed most of the men in her accounting firm, yet she was denied a partnership. One of her superiors urged her to "walk more femininely, talk more femininely, dress more femininely, wear make-up, have her hair styled, and wear jewelry" (Fiske et al., 1991, p. 1050). With the help of social psychologist Susan Fiske, who gave expert testimony on her behalf, Hopkins was able to convince the Supreme Court that the company had discriminated against her.

The gap between men's and women's salaries is also substantial. Even when men and women do the same job, women's wages are 65 to 68% of men's wages. Do men work harder than women? Are they more productive? Do they have better credentials? No. When differences in work quality, absenteeism, or educational level are taken into account, the gap remains. The man with a college degree who takes 2 weeks of vacation, misses 7 days of work due to sickness, and brings in $200,000 worth of business for his company will be

▲ **TABLE 7-3**
Summing up: Forms of prejudice against women in contemporary society

Form of Prejudice	*Impact on Women*
Stereotypes	People perceive men and women in stereotypical ways. Women are viewed as emotionally expressive, whereas men are expected to be more instrumental. Stereotypes also suggest that certain occupations and roles are more appropriate for one sex rather than the other.
Evaluations	The qualities that comprise traditional stereotypes about women are not as positive as the qualities incorporated in stereotypes about men. Actions and accomplishments are evaluated less positively when attributed to women than to men. Roles traditionally filled by women are considered to be less important than roles occupied by men.
Economic bias	Women are underrepresented in many occupations, and their advancement through the ranks in business is slower than that of men. Women are paid 68% of what men are paid for identical work.
Victimization	Women, more so than men, are the targets of sexual harassment, domestic violence, incest, and rape. Their personal freedoms are restricted.

paid $50,000, whereas the woman with exactly the same profile would be paid, on average, $34,000 (Statistical Abstract of the United States, 1992).

Sexism even influences women's health and well-being. Women who work outside the home often experience more stress than men because they continue to do more of the domestic chores (Biernat & Wortman, 1991). Women are more likely to experience sexual harassment and its stressful consequences (Fitzgerald, 1993). Women tend to be the victims of violence, whereas men tend to be the perpetrators of violence. How many women who are murdered in the United States are killed by their husbands or boyfriends: a shocking 29%! How many men are murdered by their wives or girlfriends: 4%. Women are usually the victims in cases of domestic violence, just as they are more frequently the victims of rape. Hence, women are not as free as men are even today. Men can more freely choose when and where they will go than women can (Nielsen, 1990):

> In some life-sustaining situations, the assurance of civil rights remains problematic for women. . . . If we also take into consideration statistics on rape (most victims are female), incest (most cases are man-girl), and other forms of physical or psychological violence primarily against women (e.g., sexual harassment), there is a widespread pattern of men using physical force to control, coerce, intimidate, or otherwise limit women. (p. 59)

Prejudice in America: Conclusions

Despite decades of political and social activism, prejudice—and its pernicious consequences—persists. Many blacks in America continue to suffer indignities and disadvantages that whites do not. Most African Americans feel that they have "little or no power" in American society, and that whites' racist attitudes create barriers for them that are difficult to overcome. The strength of blacks' personal convictions has helped them cope with these social inequities, but many of the advances achieved during the 1960s and 1970s have eroded in the 1980s (Institute for Social Research, 1983; Sigelman & Welch, 1991). Similarly, sexism remains ubiquitous (see Table 7-3). Although many fields are now open to women, their wages remain about 68% of the amount paid men working similar jobs. Women are also overrepresented in low-status occupations and underrepresented in more prestigious positions (Eagly & Steffen, 1984). These status differences reinforce stereotypes about men and women and may contribute to feelings of inadequacy in women. As Geraldine Ferraro (1984) explains, for "every woman who endures the degradation and self-doubt that result from being paid less than she is worth," the gap between men's and women's wages "is an issue of human dignity" (p. 1166).

Sources of Prejudice

In *The Nature of Prejudice,* Gordon W. Allport (1954) laments the sad state of humanity. Even though we have achieved great technological feats and have cured many devastating diseases, the human race remains burdened by unwarranted animosities:

> Moslems distrust non-Moslems. Jews who escaped extermination in Central Europe find themselves in the new State of Israel surrounded by anti-Semitism. Refugees roam in inhospitable lands. Many of the colored people of the world suffer indignities at the hands of whites who invent a fanciful racist doctrine to justify their condescension. (p. ix)

Why do we seek esteem and acceptance from others but deal out rejection in return? What are the sources of prejudice?

Psychological Sources

We can't ignore the intensity of Boyle's reaction to Booker. He did not just think to himself, "A black man; he's not as good as I am." He attacked Booker because Booker was an African American. His reaction was so extreme, so irrational, that it suggests that deep-seated but powerful psychological processes sustained his bigotry. This interpretation, which owes much to Sigmund Freud's thinking, hypothesizes that Boyle broadcast his own self-hatred, frustration, and personality flaws when he belittled others (Ostow, 1991).

Prejudice as ego defense. Prejudice against African Americans is greatest among whites of low socioeconomic status (Pettigrew, 1978). People who feel insecure about their own abilities are more likely to judge others harshly (Amabile & Glazebrook, 1982). Men who are low in self-acceptance are more attracted to women who conform to gender stereotypes (Grube, Kleinhesselink, & Kearney, 1982). People who have just experienced a blow to their self-esteem are more likely to discriminate against others than are people who have just gone through an esteem-bolstering experience (Hogg & Sunderland, 1991). When we are reminded of our mortality—that we won't live forever—we become less tolerant toward people who don't accept our worldview (Greenberg et al., 1992). Why?

Individuals who feel threatened and uncertain about their own status and worth sometimes defend their egos by attitudinally rejecting others. As shown in Chapter 6, attitudes fulfill various functions for people, including ego defense. The man who worries about his own masculinity and competency may mask his lack of self-confidence by criticizing women. The white job applicant who fails to land the job can rationalize this failure by expressing hatred for blacks. In general, whites who feel that they are being surpassed economically, socially, and politically by blacks are strongest in their rejection of blacks (Bobo, 1983; Doty, Peterson, & Winter, 1991; Vanneman & Pettigrew, 1972).

▲ A sexist man would be unlikely to support Lynn Yeakel's bid for election to the U.S. Senate. An ego-defensive explanation of this rejection argues that his opposition may stem from his own feelings of inadequacy or failure. Troubled by these unrecognized self-doubts, he responds by lashing out at women who are more successful than he is.

Prejudice as scapegoating. What kind of day did Boyle have the day he accosted Booker? Did he get a parking ticket? Did his boss call him into the office and tell him to improve his work performance? Did he argue with his girlfriend?

scapegoat theory of prejudice
An explanation of conflict between racial groups that argues hostility caused by frustrating environmental circumstances is sometimes released by taking hostile actions against members of other social groups.

The **scapegoat theory of prejudice** argues that tensions build up in people when they experience frustrations, and these tensions must eventually find release. When people like Boyle fight with their girlfriends, are criticized by their bosses, or are reminded that their chances for a prosperous life are next to nil, they sometimes respond by attacking people who have nothing to do with their situations. These scapegoats are not the sources of the individuals' misfortunes, but they serve as outlets for frustrations when hostility toward the actual frustrator is blocked.

The scapegoat theory explains why frustrating economic conditions often stimulate increases in prejudice and violence. Studies of anti-black violence in southern areas of the United States between 1882 and 1930 indicate that outbreaks of violence tended to occur whenever the economy of that region worsened (Hovland & Sears, 1940). Indeed, the correlation between the price of cotton (the main product of that area at the time) and the number of lynchings of black men by whites ranged from −0.63 to −0.72, suggesting that when whites were frustrated by the economy, they took out their frustrations by attacking blacks (see also Mintz, 1946, for a more sophisticated analysis of the Hovland-Sears data). Similar explanations have been offered to account for riots that began in the 1960s and have carried through to the Los Angeles riots of the 1990s. Even though African Americans are angered by their mistreatment by employers, property owners, and police, they can not express their hostility through direct attacks on these groups. They therefore vent their hostility by attacking scapegoats—shop owners, passing motorists, and firefighters—rather than the source of their frustrations (Harding et al., 1969).

Prejudice as a personality trait. What was Boyle like, as a person? Was he a nonconformist, or did he have respect for middle-class American values? Did he comply when his boss told him to tuck in his shirt? Was he sentimental? Did he enjoy exerting authority over others? What are the typical personality characteristics of a prejudiced person?

A team of researchers investigated this question at the University of California at Berkeley in the 1940s (Adorno et al., 1950). Responding to the flood of anti-Semitism (prejudice against Jews) sweeping Nazi Germany, these researchers explored the personalities of highly prejudiced persons through in-depth interviews, clinical case studies, and questionnaires. Their analyses revealed a distinctive pattern of values and beliefs that researchers labeled the **authoritarian personality**. The three most important earmarks of authoritarianism are listed in Table 7-4. First, authoritarians tend to be high in *conventionality*. They feel that the status quo should be maintained at all costs and that conventional social standards should not be challenged. Second, they display signs of *respectful submission* to authority; they believe that children should mind their parents and that obedience is a virtue. Third, authoritarians endorse *punitive aggression* as a means of dealing with many social problems. They believe that the "world is a dangerous place" and that people should be punished harshly when they do things that threaten society's values (Altemeyer, 1981, 1988, p. 146).

authoritarian personality
An overall system of values, beliefs, and preferences characterized by conventionalism (adherence to traditional social values), respectful submission (uncritical acceptance of authority), and aggression (hostile rejection of nonconformists).

The Berkeley researchers measured authoritarianism with a questionnaire that they called the **F-scale**; *F* because high scorers tended toward fascist political and social values. This scale has been used in hundreds and hundreds of studies, yet its meaning remains controversial (Christie, 1991). However, the basic premise of this approach to prejudice—that some attitudes are deeply rooted in the individual's personality—has been supported in a wide range of studies. Authoritarians, for example, tend to be very envious of people who are successful in school or in business, and they are more likely to express satisfaction when these "tall poppies" fail (Feather, 1993). They are also more likely to view people with AIDS, the homeless, and homosexuals as members of the outgroup who should be punished. They tend to agree to such statements as "They should quarantine everyone with AIDS, just like they would do with the plague or chicken pox," "AIDS is a plague that homosexuals pass on to the decent people," and "The homeless are basically lazy" (Peterson, Doty, & Winter, 1993, pp. 182–183; Witt, 1989). Other studies have linked authoritarianism with prejudice against blacks (Schuman, Bobo, & Krysan, 1992), right-wing political attitudes (Altemeyer, 1988), obedience to authority (Milgram, 1974), and an intolerance of new political ideas (McFarland, Ageyev, & Abalankina-Paap, 1993). These findings suggest that some people, given the nature of their personalities, are prone to be prejudiced against others.

F-scale
A self-report measure of authoritarianism, so named because high scorers tend to adopt extremely conservative (fascistic) political views.

▲ **TABLE 7-4**
Three basic components of the authoritarian personality

Component	*Interpretation*
Conventionalism	Rigid adherence to traditional social values and standards of behavior; uncomfortable with people or ideas that violate conventional values
Respectful submission	Uncritical acceptance of authority; emotional need to submit to others who are dominant or powerful
Authoritarian aggression	Feelings of hostility and anger; condemnation of anyone who violates conventional norms

Source: Adorno et al., 1950.

▲ Social categorization prompts us to classify people into groups. One of the most basic distinctions made is "in my group" and "not in my group." Michael, the boy in the cartoon, categorizes differently than his mother does: he notices age rather than race.

Cognitive Sources

We are a thinking, reasoning species. When we meet someone for the first time, we rush to put them into a *category* where their idiosyncratic qualities are soon forgotten. We also use *stereotypes* to round out our impressions when specific information about a person is sketchy. These mental abilities, although undeniably adaptive in the long run, nonetheless provide a cognitive foundation for our prejudices. As Allport (1954) concluded, "Given a thimbleful of facts we rush to make generalizations as large as a tub" (p. 9).

Social categorization. As Chapter 3 explains, we are categorizers. When we see a feathered animal that flies, we assign it to the category "birds." If we trip over a piece of granite, we might say to ourselves "Ah, an igneous rock." And, in Boyle's case, if he meets a young man on a dark city street who has more pigment in his skin than he does, he puts him in the category "black." Categorization is, in all likelihood, an automatic cognitive process; without much effort we rapidly pigeonhole the people we encounter each day. But once we fit people into a category, we no longer look at them as separate people with unique qualities. The individual is recognized as a member of our group—the ingroup—or as a member of some other group—the outgroup (Messick & Mackie, 1989; Stephan, 1985).

When we decide someone is one of "those people," we look at him or her in a different way. They lose their individuality and become more similar to other people in their group—at least in our eyes. This tendency is called the *outgroup homogeneity bias,* for it leads to the erroneous belief that people in other groups possess similar qualities and characteristics. Women's descriptions of men, for example, are less variable than their descriptions of women. Physics majors assume dance majors are all alike, but they think of physics majors as a hodgepodge of different types. Students at Princeton consider Rutgers students to be all cut from the same cloth, but they deem Princeton students to be a diverse lot.

The outgroup homogeneity bias may even lead to errors in recognizing people in other groups. We have a remarkable ability to identify faces we have seen, but our accuracy diminishes when we must make judgments about people in other racial groups (Brigham, 1986; Brigham et al., 1982). In one study, people from various racial groups looked at 20 photographs of people from their racial groups or from other racial groups. When they were tested a minute later, people were much more likely to recognize members from their own racial group than people from other groups. Whites had trouble recognizing blacks, blacks had trouble recognizing whites and Asians, and Asians had trouble recognizing whites (Luce, 1974). Other evidence suggests that we have the capability of distinguishing people from other groups. When, for example, we see a person from another group, we can intuitively appraise his or her attractiveness or friendliness, just as we appraise members of our own group (Zebrowitz, Montepare, & Lee, 1993). Yet we don't always live up to our capabilities (Anthony, Copper, & Mullen, 1992). Many different types of people may belong to a group, yet we conclude that "they all look alike to me" (Park & Rothbart, 1982; Quattrone & Jones, 1980; Tajfel, Sheikh, & Gardner, 1964; cf. Simon & Brown, 1987).

The homogeneity bias is complemented by the *ingroup differentiation bias* (Linville, Salovey, & Fischer, 1989). Our views of other groups may be simplistic and undifferentiated, but when we turn our eye to our own group, we are struck by its diversity and complexity. Ask a man to describe men in general or a woman to characterize the typical woman and most likely they will use far more concepts and qualities than they would if they were describing the typical member of another group (Linville, 1982; Linville & Jones, 1980; Park & Rothbart, 1982; Quattrone, 1986).

Our judgments about people aren't necessarily more negative once they have been categorized, but they do tend to become more extreme. A white bystander, for example, might say that Boyle (who was white) seemed "angry," but that Wilson (who was black) was "scared to death." A black bystander, in contrast, would say that Boyle was "furious," whereas Wilson was "frightened." In one study of this *extremity bias,* college-age men read a favorable or unfavorable story about a person who was not in their age group (an elderly person) or a person who was in their age group (a young person). When they later rated the person in the stories they had read, they rated the older person more positively when the story was favorable and more negatively when the story was unfavorable (Linville, 1982). Categorizing people can polarize our opinions of them.

The racially toned phrase, "You seen one, you seen them all," illustrates another category-based bias: the tendency to make sweeping statements about the entire outgroup after observing one or two of the group's members. If a black is victimized by a white employer, he or she may decide that all whites are racists. Similarly, a visitor to another country who is treated rudely by a passerby may leap to the conclusion that everyone who lives in that country is discourteous. We fall prey to the **law of small numbers** whenever we assume that the behavior of a large number of people can be accurately inferred from the behavior of a few people.

law of small numbers
The tendency for people to base sweeping generalizations about an entire group on observations of a small number of individuals from that group.

Even students at such prestigious universities as Rutgers and Princeton aren't immune to this bias. Men recruited from these schools watched a videotape of a student making a simple decision, such as deciding to wait alone or with others before the start of an experiment. They then estimated how many other students would make the same choice as the person on the videotape. Students obeyed the law of small numbers when they were initially uncertain about how most people would react (see Figure 7-8). When they thought they were watching a student from another school, they used this single person as a guide for estimating the entire group's response. If, for example, the Rutgers student saw a Princeton student decide to wait alone, he then decided that most Princeton students would want to wait alone. When they thought they were watching a student from their own school, however, they were more conservative in estimating how many people would make the same decision (Quattrone & Jones, 1980).

The opposite process—assuming that the characteristics of a single individual in a group can be inferred from the general characteristics of the whole group—can also lead us astray. If we know our group's position on an issue, we

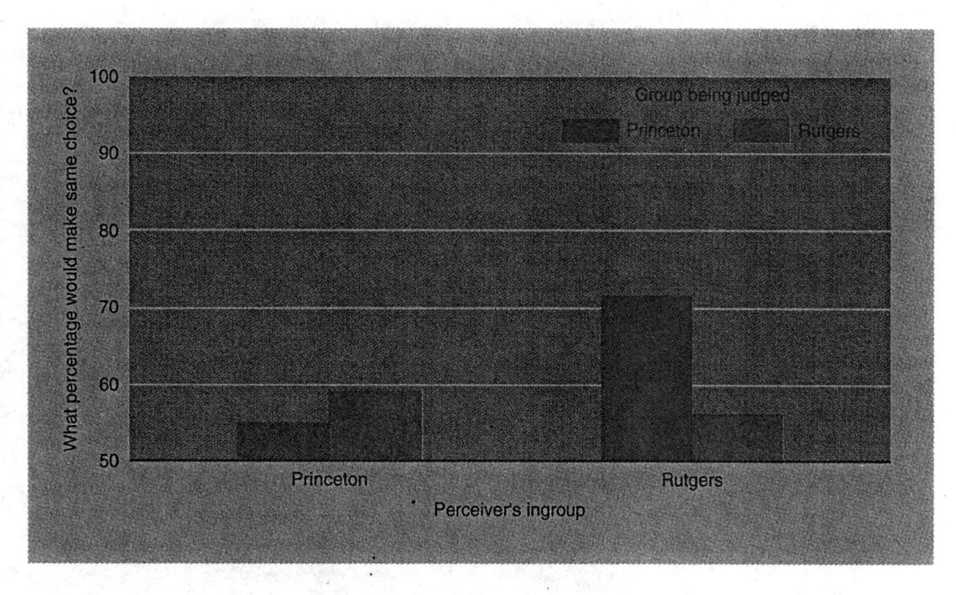

▲ **FIGURE 7-8**
Do people intuitively believe the racist phrase, "You seen one, you seen 'em all"? When Rutgers students watched a Princeton student make a choice, they assumed that most Princeton students would make the same choice as the person they watched. The Princeton students, to a lesser degree, showed the same tendency to infer the entire group's choice after seeing one individual make a choice. (Data from Quattrone & Jones, 1980)

are reluctant to assume any one of us agrees with the majority. When we know another group's position, however, we are much more willing to assume each person in that group agrees with that position. Scott Allison and his colleagues studied **group attribution error** by telling their college-student subjects that an election had recently been held at their college or at another college to determine how much funding should be given to the colleges' athletics programs. They then told the students the results of the vote, and asked them to estimate the opinion of the "typical student" at the college where the vote was taken. When the students thought the vote had been taken at their own college, they didn't want to assume that the individual's opinion would match the group's opinion. But when they thought the vote was taken at another college, they were much more confident that the individual's opinion would match the group's opinion (Allison & Messick, 1985; Allison, Worth, & King, 1990).

group attribution error
The tendency for perceivers to assume that individual group members' beliefs and characteristics can be inferred from their group's decisions and general characteristics.

Stereotyping. Stereotyping goes hand in hand with the categorization processes summarized in Table 7-5. Once we classify a person into a group, we assume that they will possess the qualities and characteristics that typify people in that group. Stereotypes are not intrinsically prejudicial. Like all cognitive schemas, stereotypes summarize large amounts of information about other people, structure our perceptions of others, and reduce the load placed on our fallible memories (Judd & Park, 1993; Macrae, Milne, & Bodenhausen, 1993; Swim, 1994). Unlike many other schemas, however, stereotypes are widely adopted by many people rather than by single individuals (Simon, Glässner-Bayerl, & Stratenwerth, 1991). They also tend to be exaggerated rather than accurate, negative rather than positive, and resistant to revision even when we encounter individuals who directly disconfirm them (Stephan & Rosenfield, 1982). We cling to our stereotypes so resolutely that they become unreasonable beliefs rather than honest misconceptions. Allport (1954) writes: "prejudgments become prejudices only if they are not reversible when exposed to new knowledge" (p. 8).

If stereotypes have all these perceptual and cognitive limitations, why do they persist? Walter Lippmann (1922), who first used the word *stereotype* to describe our intuitive assumptions about people, argued that the stereotype resists disconfirmation because "it stamps itself upon the evidence in the very

▲ TABLE 7-5
Summing up: Categorization processes in social perception

Process	Description	Common Expression
Outgroup homogeneity bias	People assume that individuals in other groups all possess similar qualities and characteristics.	"They all look alike to me."
Ingroup differentiation bias	People think their own group is complex and diverse.	"We are all individuals who can't be easily described."
Extremity bias	People are more extreme when making judgments about people in other groups.	"We are thrifty, but they are miserly."
Law of small numbers	People assume that valid judgments about another group can be based on observations of a small number of individuals from that group.	"You seen one, you seen them all."
Group attribution error	People assume that valid judgments about individuals can be inferred from the general characteristics of the whole group.	"He (or she) is just like all the rest."

act of securing the evidence." When we see people through eyes clouded by stereotypes, we misperceive and misremember people and events. Yet only rarely do we notice these errors, for our stereotypes are protected by confirmatory biases that serve to affirm their validity.

We sometimes reinterpret ambiguous information so that it matches our expectations. Prejudiced white people, for example, when asked to make up a story about a picture of a black person interacting with a white person, usually assumed the whites and blacks were arguing with one another, and they usually blamed the black for starting the dispute (Allport & Postman, 1947). White college students who observed a staged argument between a black and a white in which one person shoved the other described the push as "violent" when the perpetrator was black, but "playing" or "dramatizing" when the perpetrator was white (Duncan, 1976). Junior high school boys described the actions committed by a black male in a drawing as "meaner" and more threatening than the identical behavior performed by a white male (Sagar & Schofield, 1980). Stereotypes resist disconfirmation because we reinterpret the evidence until we see what we expect. (See Chapter 3 for more information about the complex relationship between our schemas, expectations, and perceptions.)

Stereotypes also influence what we remember and forget. The white parking lot attendant remembered that Wilson had shouted "Dig him" during the fight. Anti-black teachers may not remember how many white students failed the last test, but they may clearly remember how many black students failed. The person who believes that accountants are timid and waitresses are loud won't remember the extraverted accountant but will remember the boisterous waitress (Hamilton & Rose, 1980). People even forget the negative behaviors that members of their own group performed but recall with great acumen the objectionable actions undertaken by people in other groups (Howard & Rothbart, 1980; Park & Rothbart, 1982; Rothbart et al., 1978; Rothbart, Evans, & Fulero, 1979). These stereotype-based memory

illusory correlations Assumed relationships between two variables that are not related to one another; for example, erroneously assuming that a certain characteristic (such as skin color) is related to some other characteristic (such as hostility).

biases have been implicated as one of the key causes of **illusory correlations**: overestimations of the strength of the relationship between unrelated characteristics. (For more information, see the section, "In Depth: Illusory Correlations and Misperceptions.")

Interpersonal processes also insulate our stereotypes from disconfirmation. When we interact with others, we tend to evoke new behaviors in those persons that are consistent with our stereotype-based expectations. Allport (1954) describes an Irishman and a Jew who

> encounter each other in casual contact, perhaps in a small business transaction. Neither has, in fact, any initial animosity toward the other. But the Irishman thinks, "Ah, a Jew; perhaps he'll skin me; I'll be careful." The Jew thinks, "Probably a Mick; they hate the Jews; he'd like to insult me." With such an inauspicious start both men are likely to be evasive, distrustful, and cool. (p. 252)

Allport's anecdote suggests that stereotypes can function as *self-fulfilling prophecies* (see Chapter 3). If Boyle thinks that black people are dangerous, he may keep his eye on Booker when their paths cross. But Booker may see the suspicion in Boyle's eyes and react negatively. Boyle takes Booker's reactions as evidence that his suspicions are correct, so he challenges him. This cycle of expectation and behavioral confirmation continues until the prophecy of conflict is fulfilled (Cooper & Fazio, 1986).

One team of researchers examined this cycle of self-fulfilling prophecy in two studies of racism. In the first, white male college students interviewed white and black high school students who were interested in joining a team. The interviewers were not aware that the high school students had been trained to give certain answers and behave in a standard fashion. Despite the similarity in their actions, the white interviewers treated black interviewees more negatively than white interviewees: they sat farther away from them, displayed signs of nervousness, and terminated the interviews sooner.

Now the researchers took the situation one step further by asking, How will people react when they encounter an interviewer who displays these negative behaviors? All the subjects in this second study were white, but some encountered an interviewer who enacted the negative behaviors identified in the first study. Others met with an interviewer who treated them in a more positive manner. In essence, some of the subjects were treated like whites, and others were treated like blacks.

When an independent panel of judges rated their performance, the whites who were treated negatively (the way blacks were in the first study) were judged to be less competent, less confident, and generally less desirable as employees. The whites who were treated like the whites in the first study were rated more favorably. These findings argue that in an actual interview the interviewee will probably live up (or down) to the interviewer's stereotypical beliefs (Word, Zanna, & Cooper, 1974; see also Lord & Saenz, 1985; Skrypnek & Snyder, 1982).

Interpersonal Sources

Boyle didn't develop racist attitudes all by himself. His personality and cognitive outlook may have fed his enmity toward blacks, but interpersonal processes undoubtedly supported these personal processes as well. Growing up in the United States, he could not have avoided socializing forces that condone racism or ignored social norms that call for the differential treatment of people based on their race, sex, or ethnicity.

Illusory Correlations and Misperceptions

The white racist thinks that being black and being lazy go together. The sexist assumes that most women are manipulative. The homophobic is certain that homosexuality is linked to promiscuity. What factor sustains these illusory correlations—the tendency to see relationships between qualities that are totally unrelated to each other?

Studies of our powerful, but occasionally prejudiced, memory systems offer some answers. In an early investigation of memory errors, researchers read people long lists of word pairs, such as *lion-tiger, blossoms-notebook,* and *bacon-eggs.* Even though each word was paired with every other word an equal number of times, people insisted that common pairings, such as *bacon-eggs,* occurred more frequently than uncommon pairs (for example, *lion-eggs*). They also believed that distinctive words were more frequently paired. The words *blossoms* and *notebook,* for example, were longer than most of the other words, and many subjects overestimated the number of times these two words were paired (Chapman, 1967; Chapman & Chapman, 1967).

Social psychologist David Hamilton and his colleagues are now convinced that both of these kinds of memory biases combine to produce illusory correlations in our judgments of other people. Do you think that accountants are timid? Do you believe that women make good business leaders? To answer these kinds of questions, you must sift through your memories about accountants and women bosses to determine how many did and did not have these particular qualities. This judgment process will be biased, however, when your stereotypes about these groups expedite the recall of confirming instances while obstructing the recall of disconfirming instances (Hamilton, 1979; Hamilton & Gifford, 1976; Hamilton & Rose, 1980; Hamilton & Sherman, 1989; Stroessner, Hamilton, & Mackie, 1992).

Hamilton's research group examined this process by asking students to read a long list of statements describing various people. The statements included a person's name, his or her occupation, and two adjectives. "Ed, the accountant, is timid and talkative" and "June, the stewardess, is wealthy and attractive" are examples. Unknown to subjects, the adjectives were paired with each occupational group an equal number of times. There were as many timid accountants in the list as there were timid stewardesses. Yet, when Hamilton tested their memory by asking them to recall how many times a particular adjective such as *timid* or *attractive* was used to describe accountants and stewardesses, they overestimated the number of timid accountants and attractive stewardesses because those pairings matched their stereotype-based expectations (Hamilton & Rose, 1980). They saw a correlation between variables that were actually unrelated to each other (McArthur & Friedman, 1980).

Differences in the frequency of cases can also set the stage for illusory correlations. Imagine that you see a woman flight attendant spill coffee on a passenger. Even though this action is distinctive—you don't often see flight attendants fumble in their duties—the person who did the fumbling isn't distinctive—most flight attendants are women. What if the flight attendant had been a man? In this case, two rare events would have been linked, and they would therefore have become easier to recall. If you were asked whether men or women make better flight attendants, you would be more likely to remember the clumsy man and to state that women make better flight attendants.

Hamilton's research group examined the impact of shared distinctiveness on illusory correlations directly by giving subjects a list of 39 statements, such as "Ed, who is in Group A, complimented a stranger." Each statement included the person's name, their group membership (either A or B), and a description of either a positive or negative behavior. Negative behaviors were relatively rare: 12 of the 39 (31%) actions were negative, but 27 (69%) were positive. However, members of group B were also rare. The set of 39 statements included 26 descriptions of Group A, but only 13 statements about Group B. Hamilton made certain that the group membership did not covary with behaviors. The proportion of members of Group A who performed bad behaviors was equal to the proportion of members of Group B who performed bad behaviors. But when subjects' memories were tested later, they attributed more negative behaviors to the smaller group—Group B—than Hamilton had actually shown them. He concluded that, because Group B and bad behaviors were both infrequent, they were also more distinctive to perceivers (Hamilton & Gifford, 1976).

Hamilton's findings explain why stereotypes about minority groups tend to take on a negative tone rather than a positive one. Members of minority groups, by definition, are rarer, and therefore more distinctive. Moreover, negative events, traits, and behaviors are also more distinctive than positive events, traits, and behaviors. Hence, we tend to overestimate the covariation between negative qualities and minority group members. A white person may encounter 10 blacks and 40 whites during a typical day because whites outnumber blacks. But if 2 blacks and 8 whites display negative qualities, such as the use of offensive language or rudeness, the perceiver will still overestimate the correlation between skin color and negative characteristics. We may not want to view others in stereotyped ways, but our limited ability to process information completely sometimes distorts our perceptions anyway (Hamilton & Sherman, 1989; Mullen & Johnson, 1990).

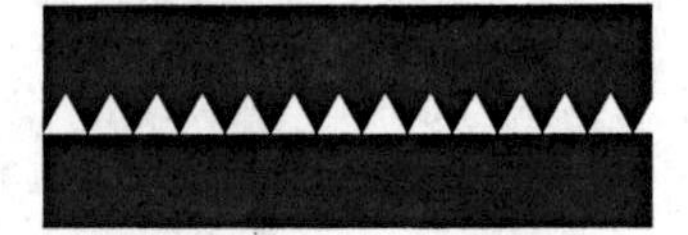

▲ Symbolic cues in the media and in advertisements define the relative value of men and women. This display of advertisements is rich with meaning. The man's image is placed above the woman's. He is dressed, whereas the woman is wearing only a bathing suit. Notice, too, the "faceism" in the two ads: the billboard featuring the man focuses on his head and upper torso, whereas the ad featuring the woman shows her entire body.

Social learning. Boyle wasn't born a bigot. Rather, as he grew up in a racially mixed society, he probably acquired his negative opinions about blacks from other people. Prejudiced parents often pass their biases on to their children. They may explicitly tell children that other groups are inferior, and forbid them from playing with them. Some parents reward children who express sexist or racist beliefs, and punish those who fail to adopt their values. Moreover, as social learning theory predicts, when parents act in ways that are prejudicial, their children tend to imitate these prejudices (Carlson & Iovini, 1985; Milner, 1983).

Peers are another significant source of prejudice. Perhaps Boyle was originally neutral toward African Americans, but after spending time with Cuneo, he may have adopted his friend's racist attitudes (Bagley & Verma, 1979; Patchen, 1982). Boyle may have also learned to be prejudiced through exposure to negative images of blacks and women in books, newspaper stories, advertisements, television programs, and cartoons. Blacks are underrepresented in children's books, comics, and on television, and the few characters that do appear often conform to whites' stereotypic notions of happy-go-lucky or aggressive blacks. These biases have diminished in recent years, but even now blacks are often cast in stereotypical roles that stress sports or entertainment (Armstrong, Neuendorf, & Brentar, 1992; Branthwaite & Peirce, 1990). Bill Cosby's character, Dr. Cliff Huxtable, is a noteworthy exception, but even *The Cosby Show* failed to portray the unique and individualizing aspects of black identity (Peterson-Lewis & Adams, 1990). News reports tend to overlook instances of peaceful coexistence between the races to highlight cases of racial conflict (Milner, 1983). Television programs also continually use the color white as a symbol of goodness and the color black as a symbol of evil (Duckitt, 1992; Elliot & Tyson, 1983).

Sexism, too, can be traced back to the symbolic cues that subtly define the value of men and women. Through the newspapers we learn that the world's affairs are shaped mostly by men. Many advertisements in magazines depict women as subservient to men and overly concerned with their physical appearance. Moreover, photographs of women in magazines often focus on their bodies, whereas photographs of men tend to center on their faces. This "faceism" sends the implicit message that women are judged by the shapes of their bodies, and men are judged by the strength of their ideas (Archer et al., 1983; Copeland, 1989).

▲ So why is it that the characters in cartoons and comics tend to be male rather than female? Does it reflect society's tendency to favor men over women?

Women, like blacks, are also portrayed in stereotyped ways on television. Even though more and more women are working outside the home, in commercials they are most often depicted as housewives. Studies of commercials indicate that women are often portrayed as unintelligent, dependent on male advice, incapable of performing simple tasks, easily persuaded, eager to please men, envious of women who are better cooks or housekeepers, devoted to traditional roles of parenting, and deeply concerned with maintaining their attractiveness (Davis, 1990; Russo, Feller, & DeLeon, 1982). During sports broadcasts, commercials become more stereotypical, but prime-time commercials portray both sexes more fairly (Craig, 1992). Men outnumber women 3 to 1 in the world of television. Researchers identified 986 characters in 115 TV episodes broadcast during a two-week period. They found that 64.9% of the characters were male, and that 67.7% of the people who were portrayed in occupations were men (Vande-Berg & Streckfuss, 1992). When an off-screen voice introduces a product during a commercial, 89.9% of the time the voice is a man's rather than a woman's (Lovdal, 1989). Victims of violence are usually women rather than men (Huston et al., 1992). Most music videos feature men rather than women, and the women who do appear often seem passive and aimless (Brown, 1985). Four percent of the males, but over 30% of the females, in music videos broadcast by MTV wore revealing clothes (Seidman, 1992). Given all these prejudicial cues, it is not surprising that children who are not already sexist tend to become so if they watch large amounts of television (Gunter, 1986; Huston et al., 1992; Signorielli, 1989).

Norms and prejudice. The air force officer finds himself surrounded by people who ridicule women pilots. He begins to agree with them. Cuneo may not be prejudiced against blacks, but when he's with Boyle he goes along with his buddy's plan to harass them. The Alabama native is prejudiced against blacks, but when she goes to college in California her biases fade.

The officer, Cuneo, and the student are all responding to social norms—consensual standards that describe what behaviors should and should not be performed in a given situation. As we examine in more detail in Chapter 9, norms guide our actions in all manner of social settings. Why do you wear a particular style of clothes, eat three meals a day, smile when others smile at you, and value hard work? Because norms structure your actions and attitudes. In some of these situations, you may be following the norm just to avoid sanctions or to seem agreeable. But when you internalize a norm, it becomes a part of your total value system. You don't work hard just because you want to conform to social norms but because working hard is personally satisfying.

But can something as elusive as a social norm cause something so pervasive as prejudice? Research clearly says it can. Thomas Pettigrew (1958, 1959, 1960), for example, wondered whether the extreme amounts of racism seen in South Africa were caused by South Africans' personality traits or by social norms that demanded separation of the black and white people. He discovered that even though South Africans were far more prejudiced than Americans, they weren't more authoritarian in their personal beliefs. He did discover, however, that white South Africans who were the most prone to conform to norms were often the most prejudiced. A person who agreed with such statements as "It's better to go along with the crowd than to be a martyr" and "Adherence to convention produces the best kind of citizen" was also more likely to express the strongest anti-black attitudes (Duckitt, 1992).

Researchers have also found that prejudicial attitudes wax and wane when people move from situations that encourage or discourage prejudice. Recall the study of racism in a small West Virginia mining town discussed in Chapter 6. The norms in the town discouraged interracial contacts and therefore promoted a high incidence of discrimination. In the mine, however, work norms emphasized cooperation and productivity, so racial discrimination was discouraged (Minard, 1952). Studies of whites who move from one geographic area to another suggest that they tend to take on new attitudes to match the standards of their new residence. Whites who moved from southern regions of the United States to northern regions became less prejudiced, whereas whites who moved to the South became more prejudiced (Middleton, 1976). Even prisoners' racial attitudes change to match the predominating racial sentiments of the institution where they are confined. One researcher identified within a single prison two housing areas that adopted different norms about interracial interaction. She then tracked changes in new inmates' attitudes when they were assigned to housing in these two areas. As Figure 7-9 indicates, over two-thirds of the inmates assigned to the section with norms favoring tolerance became less prejudiced, and over one-third of the inmates housed in the less tolerant section became more prejudiced (Foley, 1976). These findings support Allport's initial insights into prejudice and norms. In 1954 he wrote, "About a half of all prejudiced attitudes are based only on the need to conform to custom, to let well enough alone, to maintain the cultural pattern" (p. 286).

Intergroup Sources

Allport points out that prejudice is an intergroup phenomenon. It does not involve a lone individual who rejects other individuals. Rather, it involves a group of individuals who reject other groups of individuals. Boyle did not simply dislike Booker. Rather, he took pride in his whiteness and the accomplishments of his race. At the same time, he also denigrated blackness and the accomplishments of black people.

ingroup-outgroup bias The tendency to view the ingroup and its members and products more positively than the outgroup and its members and products. Ingroup favoritism is more common than outgroup rejection.

This tendency to view people in our group more favorably than those outside our group is called the **ingroup-outgroup bias**. The bias is really two biases combined: a tendency to favor our own group, its members, and products; and the tendency to derogate the outgroup, its members, and its products (Brewer, 1979; Coser, 1956; Hinkle & Schopler, 1986). In general, however, ingroup favoritism is stronger than outgroup rejection (Brewer, 1979; Coser, 1956; Hinkle & Schopler, 1986).

▲ FIGURE 7-9
Can prejudice be reduced by changing situational norms rather than individuals' attitudes? When inmates at a men's correctional facility were housed in a part of the jail with relatively positive norms about interracial contact, their prejudices abated. Many of the men who were housed in a part of the jail with anti-interracial contact norms became more prejudiced, however. (Data from Foley, 1976)

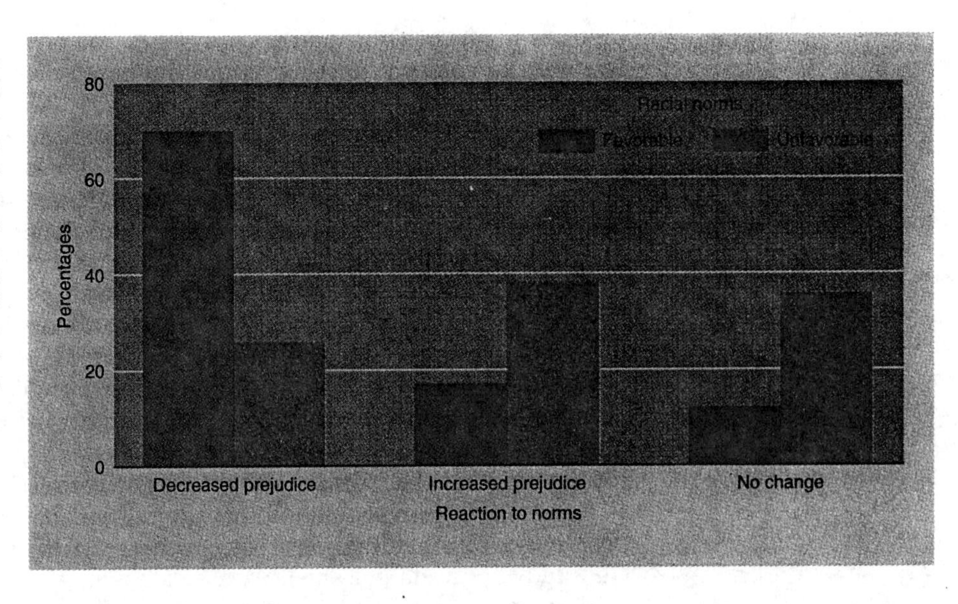

ethnocentrism
The belief that one's own tribe, region, or country is superior to other tribes, regions, or countries.

The ingroup-outgroup bias is called **ethnocentrism** when it causes tensions between members of larger social groups, such as tribes, ethnic groups, or nations. In *Folkways,* sociologist William Graham Sumner (1906) wrote:

> The insiders in a we-group are in a relation of peace, order, law, government, and industry, to each other. Their relation to all outsiders, or other-groups, is one of war and plunder. . . . Sentiments are produced to correspond. Loyalty to the group, sacrifice for it, hatred and contempt for outsiders, brotherhood within, warlikeness without—all grow together, common products of the same situation. (p. 12)

When two groups collide, the powerful intergroup processes examined next are set into motion.

Realistic group conflict. Some whites believe that blacks pose a threat to their way of life. They fear that blacks will move into their all-white suburban neighborhoods and place their children in the neighborhood schools. Whites also realize that blacks want better jobs and that they may displace white workers. Many blacks, in contrast, believe that whites strive to maintain the status quo (Institute for Social Research, 1983, p. 7).

realistic group conflict theory
A conceptual framework that argues conflict between groups stems from competition for scarce resources, including food, territory, wealth, power, natural resources, and energy.

Realistic group conflict theory claims that prejudice is caused by competition among groups over limited resources. This theory notes that the things people value, including food, territory, wealth, power, natural resources, and energy, are so limited that if the members of one group manage to acquire a scarce commodity, the members of another group will go without it. Naturally, groups would prefer to be haves rather than have-nots, so they take steps designed to achieve two interrelated outcomes: attaining the desired resources and preventing the other group from reaching its goals (Campbell, 1965; LeVine & Campbell, 1972). Groups in competition are usually groups in conflict (Rabbie & Horwitz, 1969; Rapoport & Bornstein, 1987; Taylor & Moriarty, 1987).

Realistic group conflict theory explains why the ingroup-outgroup bias emerges with a vengeance when groups compete. Groups may coexist peacefully during times of plenty, but when resources become scarce, intergroup biases escalate. Researchers in one study told some groups that they were competing with other groups. Other groups, in contrast, were told that they were cooperating with others or working independently (Worchel, Andreoli, & Folger, 1977). The groups then completed a task and were given sham feedback about their performance: Half thought they failed, and half thought they succeeded. As expected, subjects rated their own groups more favorably—the average was about 25 on the 31-point scale. The ratings of the outgroup were lower, between 19 and 20, when the two groups were cooperating or working independently, and considerably lower (the average was 15) when the groups were competing. This outgroup rejection was even more pronounced if the groups later experienced a second failure. Other studies have confirmed this effect, suggesting that ingroup favoritism is stronger than outgroup rejection and that outgroup rejection is intensified by failure (Dion, 1973, 1979; Ryen & Kahn, 1975; Wilson & Miller, 1961).

Social identity. According to the realistic group conflict theory, people become prejudiced when they feel that other groups pose a threat of some kind. Henri Tajfel and John Turner, however, argue that prejudice can occur even in the absence of conflict and threat. They believe that categorization, rather than competition, sews the seeds of conflict by creating a cognitive distinction between "us" and "them." They write, the "mere perception of belonging to two distinct groups—that is, social categorization per se—is sufficient to trigger intergroup discrimination favoring the in-group" (Tajfel & Turner, 1986, p. 13; see also Turner, 1987).

Is it possible that group membership per se—even in the absence of any competition—is sufficient to produce intergroup conflict? Tajfel and his colleagues put this hypothesis to the test in what they call the *minimal group paradigm*. They randomly assigned volunteers to one of two groups, although the volunteers were told that the division was based on some irrelevant characteristic such as art preference. Several tasks later, the subjects were then asked to divide up a small amount of money among the members of the two groups. Remember, these groups are purely cognitive; they exist in the minds of the subjects, but they have no social reality. The subjects don't know one another, can't see one another, don't expect to interact with each other, and the groups have absolutely no personal or interpersonal implications. Yet the ingroup-outgroup bias occurred nonetheless. People not only awarded more money to members of their own group, but they also seemed to try actively to keep money from members of the other group. Even when Tajfel made it clear that subjects had been assigned to the groups at random and that giving money to the outgroup would not cause any monetary loss for any ingroup member, the bias persisted. He concluded that it was the categorization process itself, rather than feelings of similarity, competition, a shared common bond, and the like, that stimulated conflict with the other group (Tajfel & Turner, 1986).

Tajfel's research provoked a search for the causes of ingroup favoritism in minimal groups that still continues (Aschenbrenner & Schaefer, 1980; Bornstein et al., 1983; Brewer, 1979; Brewer & Kramer, 1985; Hogg & Sunderland, 1991; Mason & Verkuyten, 1993). Many researchers, however, now believe that **social identity theory** offers an explanation for Tajfel's results. This theory, which draws heavily from prior social-psychological theorizing, is based on three basic assumptions. First, as the concept of social categorization maintains, we can readily distinguish between ingroup members and outgroup members. Second, we are motivated to maintain a positive social identity. Third, we derive much of our social identity from our group identities. These three assumptions, taken together, suggest that we favor members of our own

social identity theory
A conceptual explanation of prejudice that traces tensions between groups to social categorization processes (the tendency to distinguish between people who are in our group or in another group) and the need to maintain and enhance self-esteem. The theory assumes that people, by overestimating the value of their own group while derogating other groups, indirectly enhance their own self-esteem.

▲ Prejudice is an intergroup phenomenon. In this case, supporters of David Duke clash with college students who are protesting against him. Social identity theory suggests that such intergroup conflicts may indirectly enhance the group members' feelings of worth. By derogating the outgroup and revering the ingroup, individuals can find evidence of their relative superiority.

group in order to maintain and protect our own social identity. If our self-esteem is shaken by a personal setback, our group provides us with reassurance and identity (Meindl & Lerner, 1984). By praising our own group in comparison to others, we bolster our own self-esteem. By comparing our qualities to the qualities possessed by members of the outgroup, we find evidence of our superiority (Lemyre & Smith, 1985; Oakes & Turner, 1980; Turner, Sachdev, & Hogg, 1983). This explanation, although speculative, accounts for certain aspects of prejudice. For example, even though African Americans have been denied many of their civil rights and are depicted negatively in the media, they remain relatively high in self-esteem and group pride (Crocker & Major, 1989).

sociobiology
A biological approach to understanding social behavior; assumes recurring patterns of behavior in animals ultimately stem from evolutionary pressures that increase the likelihood of adaptive social actions while extinguishing nonadaptive practices.

Sociobiology of bias. The ingroup-outgroup bias is so pervasive—it is found in virtually all cultures and all eras of human history—that some experts believe it may have a genetic basis. **Sociobiology**, a branch of biology that explores the genetic roots of social behavior, suggests that favoring members of our own group and rejecting members of other groups may have given our early ancestors a distinct survival advantage. Early humans, they suggest, lived in small tribes composed of people who were genetically similar. Therefore, by helping members of one's own group, one was also helping to protect copies of one's genes that were present in these other people. Moreover, these tribes often competed violently with neighboring tribes for land, food, water, and shelter. Because outsiders were a danger, people with the ability to recognize and avoid them tended to survive, whereas those who did not tended to die off. After eons of this *natural selection* process, the earth was populated primarily by human beings with a built-in readiness to respond positively to the ingroup and negatively to the outgroup (Rushton, 1989).

Sociobiology offers a counterpoint to social psychology's emphasis on interpersonal processes as the causes of intergroup conflict (see Table 7-6). Prejudice may be an instinctive reaction to people who are unlike us genetically. Yet even sociobiology notes that biological predispositions are often strongly modified by the social situation in which the individual lives. Some aspects of our behavior may have a biological basis, but these basic patterns are not so inflexible that they cannot be altered through experience. We may instinctively react

▲ **TABLE 7-6**
Summing up: Intergroup processes that contribute to prejudice and discrimination against other groups

Process	*Characteristics*
Ingroup-outgroup bias	The tendency to favor the ingroup, its members, and its products, and the tendency to derogate the outgroup, its members, and its products. Rejection of others in larger social collectives is termed *ethnocentrism.*
Realistic group conflict	Rejection of other groups during competition for scarce resources. Members of groups that dominate other groups are less prejudiced against the outgroup than are members of groups that fail during competition with other groups.
Social identity processes	Maintaining and enhancing personal and collective self-esteem by positively evaluating the ingroup and negatively evaluating outgroups. Individuals in minimal group situations favor members of their own group even though these groups have no significance.
Sociobiology	The instinctive tendency to fear and dislike people who are unlike us genetically.

to strangers with fear and distrust, but as we see in the next section, biology's lessons can be unlearned.

Eliminating Prejudice

If prejudice were a physical disease, this pestilence could not be blamed on any one infectious germ or contagious virus. Boyle's self-doubts, his personality, his assumptions about whites and blacks, his family life, and the very existence of multiple groups in our heterogeneous society may all have played a part in making him a bigot (see Table 7-7). But this swirl of overlapping causes of prejudice also holds the key to eliminating prejudice. Because social factors sustain prejudice, perhaps these same factors can be marshalled to eliminate it.

The Contact Hypothesis

Boyle was a product of a segregated society. Growing up in Boston in the 1950s and 1960s, he had very little contact with African Americans. He never had the opportunity to work with blacks, to understand and make friends with individual members of the black community, or to forge any other interpersonal ties with blacks. The **contact hypothesis** suggests that increased contact between Boyle and blacks would have cured his prejudice: If people lived in situations that promoted frequent contact between black and white people, our prejudices would be replaced by impartiality.

contact hypothesis
The prediction that equal-status contact between the members of different groups will reduce intergroup conflict.

Muzafer Sherif and his colleagues carried out one of the best-known studies of the contact hypothesis at a boy's summer camp located in Robbers Cave State Park in Oklahoma (Sherif et al., 1961). They began their so-called **Robbers Cave Experiment** by separating 22 white 11-year-old boys into two groups: the Rattlers and the Eagles. They let the two groups solidify for a time before pitting them against one another in a series of competitions. Eventually, the researchers had to physically separate the two groups to prevent them from harming each other.

Robbers Cave Experiment
A field study performed by the Sherifs and their colleagues (1961) in an attempt to better understand the causes and consequences of intergroup conflict; the study derives its name from the state park that was the site for the research.

After creating prejudice between the two groups, the researchers then set about trying to reduce it. Hoping that contact between the groups would ease tensions, the researchers arranged for the Rattlers and the Eagles to take part

▲ **TABLE 7-7**
Summing up: Sources of prejudice

Sources	*Definition*	*Processes*
Psychological	Motivational and personality mechanisms that shift negative feelings caused by a sense of inferiority or frustration onto the members of other groups	• Ego defense • Scapegoating • Authoritarianism
Cognitive	Mental processes that facilitate social perception by making use of expectations, schemas, and other existing cognitive structures	• Social categorization • Stereotypes
Interpersonal	Social processes that facilitate the transmission of prejudicial attitudes and values from one person to the next	• Socialization • Social learning • Social norms
Intergroup	Conflict-sustaining processes that occur whenever two or more groups come into contact	• Ingroup-outgroup bias • Realistic group conflict • Social identity • Instinctive rejection of strangers

together in seven pleasant activities such as eating, playing games, viewing films, and shooting off firecrackers. Unfortunately, contact failed to cure their hostility. During all these events the lines between the two groups never broke. Pleasant experiences became rife with tension, and shared meals erupted into "food fights" and shoving matches.

The failure of contact to cure the boys' prejudices isn't surprising. When white and black schoolchildren attend the same schools, this contact doesn't necessarily reduce their prejudices. (This topic is explored in the section "Application: Reducing Prejudice Through School Desegregation," which concludes this chapter.) When rival departments in a business are moved closer together so employees must commingle during the work day, tensions between the departments don't necessarily disappear (Brown et al., 1986). College students studying in foreign countries actually become *more* negative toward their host countries the longer they remain in them (Stroebe, Lenkert, & Jonas, 1988).

Cooperation

Boyle would have probably remained prejudiced even if he had interacted regularly with African Americans. But what if the contact had occurred in a situation that required close cooperation with blacks, such as the workplace or during combat? Perhaps Boyle might have changed more if the situation had called for cooperation rather than mere contact.

The Robbers Cave Experiment provides proof of the curative contribution of cooperation over mere contact. After contact failed, the Sherifs forced the boys to work for **superordinate goals**—goals that can be attained only when groups work together. Disagreeable neighbors who unite forces when a severe thunderstorm threatens to flood their homes are working to achieve superordinate goals, as are the warring nations often depicted in science fiction who pool their technological skills to prevent the collision of the earth with an asteroid.

superordinate goals
Goals that can be attained only if the members of two or more groups work together by pooling their efforts and resources.

The Robbers Cave experimenters created superordinate goals by staging a series of crises. They secretly sabotaged the water supply so the campers awoke one morning without water. The boys became quite thirsty as they struggled to solve the problem and cheered when the problem was repaired. They told the boys that they could rent a movie, but made it clear that they could see a much more interesting movie if the two groups pooled their limited funds. When the supply truck apparently broke down, both groups of boys had to pull a shared rope to move the truck. Within days the Sherifs' efforts were rewarded: the original tensions between the groups were wiped out.

The superordinate goals were effective because, unlike the simple contact situations they created, the emergencies forced the two groups to cooperate with one another. For the preceding week, the Rattlers and the Eagles had been competitors, and this competition carried over to the simple contact situations. Even when group members tried to work with outgroup members, they earned no special rewards and were even criticized by their fellow group members. Without cooperation, the two groups continued to perceive one another as opponents who had to be rejected and defeated. They continued to discriminate against the outgroup, to view them with distrust, and even to resort to aggression and verbal abuse. When the situation called for cooperation, however, animosity was replaced by camaraderie. In general, cooperation leads to better communication, increased trust and attraction, changes in perception, and a willingness to tolerate group differences (Bodenhausen, Gaelick, & Wyer, 1987; Desforges et al., 1991; Riordan & Riggiero, 1980).

Cooperation doesn't always work, however (Worchel, 1986). First, in all likelihood several cooperative encounters will be needed before conflict is noticeably reduced. In the Robbers Cave research, a whole series of superordinate goals was required before animosity was reduced. When students from two different colleges worked together on problems, the cooperative encounter led to increased liking for members of the outgroup only when it occurred twice (Wilder & Thompson, 1980). Students who worked with the outgroup just once or not at all rated the members of the outgroup more negatively than students who worked with the outgroup twice. Similarly, in public schools a long period of cooperative intergroup contact is needed to reduce intergroup prejudice, and if cooperation is not constantly encouraged, then groups inevitably drift apart once again (Schofield, 1979; Schofield & Sagar, 1977).

Second, if the cooperative venture fails, then conflict inevitably ensues. Cooperating groups that manage to succeed like one another, but when groups fail, the negative affect associated with a poor performance spreads to the outgroup. Each group may blame the other for the misfortune, and intergroup relations may further erode. Thus, cooperation is not enough; the cooperation must also lead to success rather than failure (Blanchard, Adelman, & Cook, 1975; Blanchard & Cook, 1976; Blanchard, Weigel, & Cook, 1975; Cook, 1978, 1984; Mumpower & Cook, 1978; Weigel & Cook, 1975; Worchel & Norvell, 1980).

Undoing Categorization and Stereotyping

Norman Miller and Marilyn Brewer agree that cooperation works to dispel prejudice. They believe, however, that cooperation reduces conflict because it reverses some of the pernicious consequences of social categorization. Rather than thinking of the members of another group as "them," when working together to achieve superordinate goals, the boundary between the two groups becomes vague. Others are eventually viewed as members of our group rather than of the outgroup (Brewer & Miller, 1984; Gaertner et al., 1990; Miller & Brewer, 1986a, 1986b).

This process took place at Robbers Cave. Near the end of the project, friendships formed across the group lines, and the two groups intermingled

▲ How can this kind of interracial harmony be achieved in society at large? Researchers recommend encouraging contact between people of different races in cooperative situations.

during meals. In fact, when the researchers asked the Rattlers and Eagles if they wanted to travel home in separate buses, the boys chose a single bus. They had become Robbers Cave campers rather than Rattlers or Eagles.

Categorization can be undone in many ways. Similarities between the groups can be stressed, even if the similarities are unimportant. This technique worked well in one study when researchers asked two groups to work together on a joint task. If the researchers had the two groups wear the same color laboratory coats, then the collective effort minimized ingroup-outgroup conflict. If the two groups wore different colored coats, then the cooperative contact failed to assuage the group conflict (Worchel et al., 1978). Categorization can also be reduced by short-circuiting the outgroup homogeneity bias discussed earlier (Wilder, 1978). If people can be convinced to look at the members of the other group as individuals rather than as "them," then prejudice dwindles. When we learn that a few members of the outgroup disagree with their own group's position or have qualities that set them apart from their group, we become less likely to categorize automatically (Wilder, 1986b).

Stereotyped thinking, in contrast, has proved to be more difficult to rectify. As Patricia Devine (1989) explains, stereotyping is an automatic cognitive process. When one encounters a member of another group, or one is merely

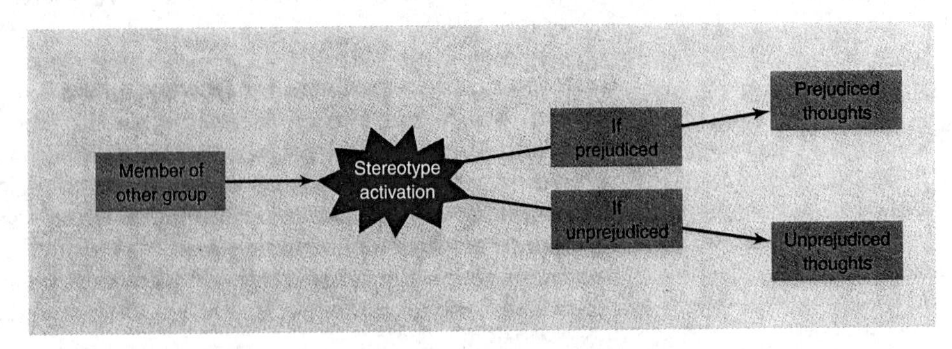

▲ **FIGURE 7-10**
Is prejudice inevitable? Patricia Devine believes that stereotypes are automatically activated when we encounter a member of another group. These stereotypes need not lead to prejudiced responses. Devine argues that unprejudiced people can't prevent stereotype activation but can inhibit its impact on thoughts, feelings, and actions. Prejudiced people cannot or do not inhibit their stereotypes.

▲ **TABLE 7-8**
Summing up: Factors that reduce prejudice and discrimination

Factor	*Characteristics*
Contact	The contact hypothesis assumes that frequent contact between groups reduces conflict between those groups. Empirical evidence (such as the Robbers Cave Experiment) does not support this hypothesis; contact per se is rarely sufficient to reduce intergroup conflict.
Cooperation	Situations that encourage groups to work together to achieve a common goal (a superordinate goal) can reduce conflict between these groups. Cooperation is most effective when it occurs repeatedly and results in successful goal attainment.
Inhibiting categorization	Conflict between groups can be eased by limiting the tendency to divide individuals into exclusive categories, such as "us" and "them." Categorization can be inhibited by emphasizing similarities rather than differences between members of different groups and by stressing each person's individual rather than group identity.
Controlling stereotyping	Stereotypes appear to be automatically activated. Unprejudiced perceivers can, however, inhibit the impact of stereotypical beliefs so that they won't influence their subsequent judgments and evaluations.

reminded of that other group by some symbol or other meaningful stimulus, stereotypes are activated. The color of a person's skin, the length of a person's hair, an accent, or a style of shoes may be enough to activate a stereotype, which may then influence our responses. Even cues that are so subtle we don't consciously recognize them may prime our stereotypes.

Devine does not believe, however, that prejudice is inevitable. Even though we may not be able to avoid the activation of stereotypes, we can control our subsequent thoughts to inhibit negative, unfair thinking (see Figure 7-10). Devine found that the whites she studied could easily list the contents of this culture's stereotypes about African Americans. She also found that whites who were low in prejudice could describe the stereotype as accurately as those who were high in prejudice. The unprejudiced whites, however, could control their thoughts after the stereotypes were activated. When asked to list their thoughts about African Americans, the unprejudiced subjects listed such things as "Blacks and whites are equal" and "It's unfair to judge people by their color—they are individuals." Prejudiced whites, in contrast, listed negative, stereotypical thoughts. Devine and her colleagues have also found that unprejudiced whites feel guilty when they find themselves responding to African Americans in stereotypical ways, whereas prejudiced whites do not (Devine et al., 1991).

Postscript on Prejudice

Is there a positive side to the social psychology of prejudice? Perhaps. By identifying the sources of prejudice, we also identify the ways to eliminate prejudice (see Table 7-8). If Boyle had experienced situations that promoted cooperation with African Americans, if he had learned to avoid categorizing people into groups based on their color, and if he had managed to inhibit his stereotyped thinking, he might be alive today.

But even though the case of Boyle and Cuneo versus Booker and Wilson ended tragically, it offers some glimmer of hope for the future. Booker went to jail for stabbing Boyle, but Wilson did not. He was charged by police with murder, but a private investigator named Gil Lewis decided to help him. Lewis was a white man, but he was not prejudiced. He did not think of Wilson as a black who had attacked a white, but instead considered him to be a person caught up in a bad situation. He arranged bail for Wilson, and together they reviewed the incident. They then searched the streets around the scene of the attack looking for witnesses and eventually found several people who could refute the police witnesses. Wilson would have surely gone to prison were it not for Gil Lewis—a white man who looked past skin color to what lies beneath the surface. People like Boyle remind us that prejudice is still a negative force in today's society, but people like Lewis reassure us that prejudice is not inevitable.

Summary

Prejudice is a powerful influence in contemporary society. The prejudiced person rejects other people simply because they belong to a disliked group. Prejudices are attitudes, so they color emotions, reinforce inaccurate *stereotypes* about people, and can lead to injurious forms of *discrimination.*

Because countless groups make up our heterogeneous society, prejudice can take many forms. *Racism,* for example, is prejudice based on race, and *sexism* is prejudice based on sex. Although *apartheid* laws that prohibited equal status contact between blacks and whites have been struck down, and few whites express racial views when interviewed by public opinion pollsters, anti-black racism persists in various forms. *Covert racism,* or public tolerance of a group paired with rejection of this group privately, surfaces when prejudiced whites feel that detection is unlikely. *Aversive racism* develops when whites accept egalitarian values but continue to experience negative emotions when interacting with blacks. *Symbolic racism* is characterized by ambivalence, for African Americans are considered to be both victims and undeserving of help. *Regressive racism* is blatant mistreatment of blacks that occurs when whites' personal prohibitions against acting in racist ways are stripped away by emotions. Stereotypes about the sexes continue to persist as well, for men and women are expected to display instrumental and expressive qualities, respectively. Moreover, the qualities, actions, accomplishments, and roles associated with women aren't as highly valued as those associated with men.

Psychological, cognitive, interpersonal, and intergroup processes combine to produce prejudice. Psychological processes, such as ego-defensiveness and scapegoating, help people avoid feelings of inferiority. The *scapegoat theory of prejudice,* for example, suggests that individuals vent their frustrations by blaming others and that those with *authoritarian personalities,* as assessed with the *F-scale,* are prone to be prejudiced against others. Social categorization and stereotyping provide a cognitive foundation for prejudice. Once we classify people into the category "them"—the outgroup—we overestimate their similarity (the homogeneity bias), overstate the ingroup's distinctiveness (the ingroup differentiation bias), make extreme judgments of outgroup members (the extremity bias), and generalize from one person to the entire group (the *law of small numbers*) and from the entire group to one individual (the *group attribution error*). Stereotypes, too, resist disconfirmation by influencing perceptions, producing *illusory correlations,* and initiating self-fulfilling prophecies.

Interpersonal processes, such as social learning and social norms, also promote prejudice. Society's socializing agents, such as our parents, peers, teachers, books, and television, teach us to reject others through direct instruction and by modeling negative attitudes. People also become more prejudiced when the situational norms condone negative attitudes and less prejudiced when norms condemn prejudice. Prejudice is also an outgrowth of conflict-sustaining processes that occur whenever two or more groups come into contact. People tend to view those in their own group more favorably than those outside their group. When this *ingroup-outgroup bias* causes conflict between larger societal groups, such as tribes or nations, *ethnocentrism* results. *Realistic group conflict theory* argues that competition for scarce resources fuels intergroup conflict, but social identity theory suggests that social categorization, per se, is sufficient to create the ingroup-outgroup bias. Analyses based on *sociobiology* go so far as to suggest that prejudice is an instinctive reaction to people who are unlike us genetically.

How can prejudice be eliminated? The *contact hypothesis* recommends promoting contact between groups, but this assumption has not been borne out by research. The *Robbers Cave Experiment* found that contact per se did not eliminate intergroup conflict, but that cooperation in the pursuit of *superordinate goals* did. Prejudice can also be undone by disabling the cognitive processes, such as categorization and stereotyping, that sustain it. Even though stereotyping appears to be an automatic process, people who are unprejudiced are able to control the impact of these negative beliefs on their subsequent judgments and evaluations. Social factors sustain prejudice, but these same factors can be marshalled to eliminate it as well.

For More Information

- *Black Americans' Views of Racial Inequality: The Dream Deferred,* by L. Sigelman and Susan Welch (1991), uses public opinion polls to develop an overall picture of African Americans' attitudes about the causes and consequences of racism in the United States.
- *The Content of Our Character,* by Shelby Steele (1990), is an articulate and insightful analysis of black-white relations in the United States.
- *The Nature of Prejudice,* by Gordon W. Allport (1954), was published in 1954, but it is still the best analysis of prejudice available. It offers an excellent integration of theory, case studies, research, and insight.
- *Opening Doors,* edited by Harry Knopke, Robert Norell, and Ronald Rogers (1991), examines prejudice from a variety of scientific and literary perspectives. The editors have included chapters by such noted experts on prejudice as John F. Dovidio, Samuel Gaertner, Thomas Pettigrew, Walter Stephan, and James Jones.
- *Psychology of Intergroup Relations,* edited by Stephen Worchel and William G. Austin (1986), includes chapters written by the leading researchers and theorists in the field. Entire chapters are devoted to such topics as social categorization, ingroup-outgroup perceptual biases, stereotypes, and inaccuracies in identifying outgroup members.
- *The Social Psychology of Prejudice,* by John Duckitt (1992), provides a comprehensive review of the causes of prejudice, with a particularly strong analysis of racism in South Africa.